# Tracing the Contours of Faith

## Christian Theology for Questioners

# Tracing the Contours of Faith

## Christian Theology for Questioners

Wayne L. Fehr

All quotes from the Bible are taken from the New Revised Standard Version, unless otherwise indicated. The following abbreviations are used for books of the Bible that are quoted:

| | | | |
|---|---|---|---|
| Gen | Genesis | Mt | Matthew |
| Ex | Exodus | Mk | Mark |
| Deut | Deuteronomy | Lk | Luke |
| Ps | Psalms | Jn | John |
| Prov | Proverbs | Acts | Acts of the Apostles |
| Isa | Isaiah | Rom | Romans |
| Ezek | Ezekiel | | |
| Dan | Daniel | 1 Cor | 1 Corinthians |
| Hos | Hosea | 2 Cor | 2 Corinthians |
| | | Gal | Galatians |
| | | Eph | Ephesians |
| | | Phil | Philippians |
| | | Col | Colossians |
| | | 1 Thess | 1 Thessalonians |
| | | 2 Tim | 2 Timothy |
| | | Heb | Hebrews |
| | | Jas | James |
| | | 1 Pet | 1 Peter |
| | | 1 Jn | 1 John |
| | | Rev | Revelation |

All references to the Book of Common Prayer (New York: Church Publishing, 1979) are indicated with the abbreviation BCP.

*Tracing the Contours of Faith*

*Copyright © 2024 Wayne L. Fehr*

Printed in the United States of America

*Wayne L. Fehr*

Wauwatosa,
WI 53213,
USA

**ISBN: (Hardcover)**
**ISBN: (Paperback)**
**ISBN: (eBook)**

# Table of Contents

# Introduction

This book is addressed to Christian believers who are feeling the ambiguities and challenges of a life of faith. Some of them are uncertain about the meaning of the faith which they profess. The familiar words that they hear in sermons and prayers seem sometimes to belong to a reality far removed from the actual world they live in. They need to discover a meaning that seems related to their own life experience and their general knowledge of the world.

To meet this kind of need, I wrote between 1999 and 2006 a monthly column called "Ask A Theologian" for the newspaper of the Episcopal Diocese of Milwaukee. Readers were invited to send in specific questions about the beliefs, doctrines and practices of the Episcopal Church, and I would attempt to answer them.

Although this material was originally written for Episcopalians, most of it is equally relevant to Christians of other traditions. I have selected the best of these columns and revised them for publication in the belief that they are worth preserving and making available to a wider readership.

I have kept the original question-and-answer format because it follows the ordinary thought processes of someone trying to understand the faith better. If theology may fairly be characterized as "faith seeking understanding" (*fides quaerens intellectum*), then the search for understanding naturally begins with a question.

The questions addressed here have arisen out of the experience of ordinary Christians trying to make sense of their faith. Some are asking about particular "Church words." Some are expressing difficulties in believing. Some are probing the paradoxes of Christian existence.

I am responding to these questions as a professional theologian writing in a non-technical way for fellow believers. My purpose is to make the best insights of sound theology available to the average believer, in order to minister to his or her faith-life. Hence, the answers given are not primarily theoretical, but are rather ordered toward the pastoral needs expressed or implied in the questions.

I have sought maximum clarity without sacrificing depth of meaning, but because of the brevity of the format, the style is fairly dense and concentrated. Hence, these pieces are best appreciated if the reader does not hurry through, but rather takes time for reflection.

The columns are grouped together according to areas of theology, but they need not be read in that order. Each essay stands alone, and is intended to be intelligible by itself. Because of the topical nature of the writing, not all relevant themes of Christian theology have been addressed.

Although many of these brief essays are limited in scope, there is a coherent understanding of Christian faith which underlies all of them. Each column is simply articulating part of that understanding in response to a specific question.

In order to give some account of my theological point of view, I need first to say a little about my own life story. My first formation in Christian faith was given to me in the American Roman Catholic Church, well before the renewal associated with the Second Vatican Council. Later, as a Catholic seminarian in the Jesuit Order in the late 1960's, I was strongly and permanently influenced by the new spirit that the Council brought.

My seminary studies in theology during those turbulent years were done in Germany, where for the first time I began to acquire a critical-historical understanding of the Bible, of Christian origins, and of the further development of the Church and its doctrines. Along with this, I absorbed the theological outlook of Karl Rahner and found that it made good sense, in a contemporary way, of the Catholic doctrines which I professed. I was ordained a Roman Catholic priest in 1969, just as the liturgical reforms mandated by the Council began to be implemented.

In 1971 I began doctoral studies in systematic theology at Yale University. There, for the first time in my education, I began to study theology in an ecumenical setting. As I got new insights from my work at Yale, I did the best I could to integrate them into the moderately liberal Roman Catholic theology I had worked out earlier.

I did my doctoral dissertation on Johann Sebastian Drey (1777-1853), a German Catholic thinker who lived and worked at a time of great creativity in Roman Catholic theology—inspired by both the

Enlightenment and the Romantic movement which followed upon it. This opened up for me yet another perspective on Catholic theology, typical of what came to be called "the Catholic Tübingen School."[1]

My own way of understanding and teaching Catholic theology was further developed and refined during the six years that I taught systematic theology at the Jesuit School of Theology in Chicago (1975-1981).

In retrospect, I can see that my way of doing theology gradually became more ecumenically and historically oriented (in contrast to traditional ways of doing Roman Catholic "dogmatic theology"). This process continued when I moved in 1982 to the faculty of theology at Marquette University in Milwaukee, where for three years I taught graduate courses and helped to administer a doctoral program, as well as teaching undergraduate courses.

Later, after leaving Marquette and the Jesuit Order, I found a spiritual home in the Episcopal Church, where I was received as a priest in 1988. As I came to know the Anglican tradition, I found much that had already become basic to my own theological method.

My way of thinking theologically is patterned by a number of values acquired through my spiritual and intellectual formation in the Roman communion. I find these also recognized and affirmed in the Anglican communion:

- Fidelity to the witness of Scripture, which embodies the historical reality of divine revelation.

- A willingness to interpret the witness of Scripture with a modern, critical-historical awareness.

- Fidelity to "the great tradition" of Christian faith through the ages, enshrined in the creeds, patristic writings, and definitions of the early ecumenical councils.

- A respect for the role of reason in theological argument and understanding.

- An openness to contemporary experience, culture, science, and philosophy.

---

1    Drey's significance for the history of Catholic theology may be assessed by consulting the author's published dissertation: Wayne L. Fehr, *The Birth of the Catholic Tübingen School: The Dogmatics of Johann Sebastian Drey* (Chico, CA: Scholars Press, 1981).

- An appreciation of "the mystical" in Christian life, and of the resources of rich spiritual traditions.

- A feeling for liturgical form and continuity of expression, celebration and ritual.

- A sense of the corporate nature of Christian faith-life, a feeling for the Body of Christ including rich human diversity in communion and mutual service.

From my further development as a professional theologian and teacher of theology, I have come to affirm, in addition, some values which modify the traditional Roman Catholic viewpoint in the direction of a more critical, open and ecumenical understanding of the Christian faith:

- An honest historical approach to Church beliefs and institutional structures.

- A willingness to let the "living tradition" continue in new and more appropriate cultural forms, by making changes and taking new initiatives.

- Freedom of speech, trusting in the power of truth to establish itself if there is open exchange of views and honest argument (in contrast to all forms of authoritarianism and paternalism).

- Respect for the cultural particularity of specific "inculturations" of Christian faith—recognizing their relative validity, willing to criticize their limitations, seeing them in relation to one another in the larger context of "the Church catholic."

My thinking arises primarily out of my lived experience as a baptized person. I recognize and acknowledge my deep indebtedness to the Roman Catholic tradition in which I underwent many years of spiritual and intellectual formation. My efforts to write about the mystery of Christ have been guided by living and praying for so many years within a liturgical and sacramental Church—first in the Roman communion and later in the Anglican communion.

The Catholic doctrinal tradition presented me with images and concepts that I have labored to understand and appreciate. In this, I have tried to re-think the doctrines in a way that is coherent with my total experience and knowledge. My advanced studies in philosophy and theology have given me intellectual resources for a fresh conceptualization of long-accepted doctrines.

I offer now a relatively brief summary of my own distinctive (though certainly not original) perspective on understanding Christian faith.

The fundamental Mystery of God is inescapable, since in it we live and move and have our being. At the limits of our human experience we sense it, but also in the heart of what is most human, when we plumb the "depth dimension" of what we are experiencing.

This Mystery has become tangible for us in a human, personal, accessible way in the reality of Jesus of Nazareth, his teachings and actions, his death, and his risen presence to the world.

Jesus is the central reality for all Christians. The "good news" about him is a message of great joy and immense consolation. Responding with an act of faith in him leads one into an ever-deepening participation in the life of the Church, the Body of Christ.

The hidden reality of the Crucified and Risen Christ is also at work, in the power of the Holy Spirit, in all human groups, cultures, and languages—forming, healing, transforming, and redeeming from evil.

At the same time, there is in the human race immense, stubborn resistance to the loving initiative of God in Christ. The world lies "in sin."

Hence the history of humankind might be regarded as a long, not-yet-finished contest between Love and the refusal to love. This is lived out in each generation, both in the social dimension and in each individual human life.

What God is doing may be understood through the symbol of "the Kingdom of God" proclaimed by Jesus. There is an order of justice, peace and true communion being constantly intended by God, continually resisted and refused by human sinfulness, but ever again taking some kind of visible shape in the midst of history. It will not be fully victorious or complete until the "end," the "consummation of all things."

The Church exists and persists as human beings are grasped by the risen Jesus in the power of the Holy Spirit, to become transformed individually and collectively, and to be formed into an organic communion of diverse persons and gifts. This Spirit-inspired fellowship is to bear witness to the Kingdom of God to the extent that it exemplifies justice, peace, and communion, and shows the fruits of the Holy Spirit.

The dynamic of the Kingdom is at work in human history wherever the Holy Spirit is (i.e., everywhere, at all times). Hence, Christians who are open to their culture will be able to recognize that dynamic wherever they encounter it, will rejoice in it, cooperate with it, and foster it (even when it is not explicitly Christian or even religious).

The Church is not separate from "the world" (i.e., the totality of human beings), but is a part of that world; it is the part which explicitly recognizes the Kingdom of God in terms of the risen Jesus and his Spirit, and which tries to live consistently according to that pattern.

The Church is not, therefore, exempt from the general reality of sinfulness that permeates the human race. It is that portion of the sinful but God-beloved world which is explicitly aware of the divine Mercy and is continually repenting and returning to the divine purposes for humankind. Repentance, forgiveness, and new beginnings are intrinsic to the life of every Church community and of every individual member.

The Church is completely human, while embodying and serving a divine reality. Hence it must go through all the growing pains, deformations, renewals, and transformations of any human community that persists in time. It must find expression in many different human cultures over centuries and even in the same time period. Hence in a real sense it is ever to be re-created by the Creator Spirit in new, heretofore unknown but wonderful and faithful forms.

"Living tradition" is a helpful concept for viewing the Church in history. There is a continuity of faith-life across generations and cultures, embodied not only in documents and rituals, but most of all in the faithful lives of individuals and communities.

A corollary of this view is the conviction that the tradition, to be alive, must continue to develop. Hence, change is not to be feared, though it must always be scrutinized closely and subjected to true spiritual discernment. This applies to theological understandings as well as practical procedures and institutional forms.

Given the difficulty of doing this kind of discernment and the inescapable limitations of human beings, there is bound to be disagreement and conflict in the history of the Church. Good people will inevitably view many things differently; hence there is always a great need for mediation, loving communication, and patient work toward mutual understanding. In this there is an important role for prudent and faithful theologians.

The work of theology is to be regarded as a "life-function of the Body," an indispensable ministry of the Church to itself. Good theological work will be characterized by "creative fidelity" to the living tradition. This kind of intellectual work will foster the continuation of the tradition by criticizing honestly any distortions or infidelities of current forms of Church belief and life, and by proposing fresh, creative interpretations of the abiding truth in dialogue with contemporary culture. The truth will emerge again in new formulations when there is sustained, open dialogue between all the voices in the Church and when all are intent upon spiritual discernment.

I consider the work of academic theology to be a shared enterprise, a work that cannot be done by any one person in isolation but only by many people in free and open interaction.

Each new initiative must be assessed by colleagues for its faithfulness to the living tradition and also for its relevance to the cultural context in which it is being formulated. New ventures should never be repressed by authority but need to be examined with professional expertise and complete honesty by the community of theologians. It often takes quite a while for a fair and adequate assessment of new attempts to understand the faith.

The Church lives in local communities of faith, made up of people who share their lives of faith regularly through various kinds of interaction, including a weekly assembly for the celebration of the Holy Eucharist.

The major source of the local faith community's vision and inspiration is Sacred Scripture. Those able to teach and preach have a special responsibility to open the treasures of Scripture for all the members, and this must be a prominent part of every liturgical celebration.

Each local Church community lives a sacramental life: initiating new members through Baptism, Confirmation, and Eucharist; renewing the personal commitment and involvement of all the members continually through regular celebrations of the Eucharist; ministering to the sick and the dying through the sacrament of anointing; celebrating marital commitments in the context of the entire community's covenant commitment to Christ in the Eucharist; providing the opportunity for the sacrament of forgiveness and reconciliation as often as it is needed; recognizing and ordaining deacons, priests and bishops to carry on the ministry of word and sacrament.

Obviously, much more than this brief summary could and should be said, if I were trying to present a comprehensive treatment of Christian faith. But I hope that this may be enough to enable readers of this collection to know from what kind of theological perspective the following essays have been written.

The kind of theological writing displayed in these essays is the author's attempt to understand and recommend some major themes of Catholic Christian theology in a way that might assist believers to live their faith better. Although it does not break ground for any new, comprehensive interpretation of the Church's faith in a systematic way, it does reflect the author's personal appropriation of the living tradition.

The reader will notice references throughout to the Anglican understanding of Christian faith. This reflects the originating context of these essays: an Episcopal priest writing for lay members of that Church. The intent of the author, however, has been to formulate understandings which can be shared widely by Christians of varying backgrounds.

An appendix includes two essays that are of interest primarily to Anglican Christians but might help any reader to assess better the point of view from which the questions in this book are treated.

# Section 1: Some Fundamental Questions

These questions fall into the area of Fundamental Theology, which addresses the very notion of God, as well as the concept of revelation and the nature of faith in God.

# Faith and Questioning

Dear Theologian,

I have a question about "faith." We are sometimes told, "Just believe!" or "Just have faith!" But what if you are being asked to accept without question some understanding of Christianity which you find questionable or dubious? Does "believing" rule out any questioning or doubt? Does it exclude any use of our intellect? How do I decide what is worthy of belief?

Doubting Thomas

Dear Thomas,

Faith, in the Biblical sense, is to place one's entire confidence and trust in God alone. Abraham exemplifies this kind of faith, and St. Paul sees the faith of Christians as a continuation of that "Abrahamic" faith. Abraham, he says, believed in *the God ... who gives life to the dead and calls into existence the things that do not exist.* And this faith *was reckoned to him as righteousness.* The same kind of faith is exemplified in Christians. *It will be reckoned to us who believe in him who raised Jesus our Lord from the dead...* (Rom 4:17, 22, 24)

Faith, in this primary and fundamental sense, is not the intellectual acceptance of propositions but rather the act (ever-renewed) of entrusting one's very self to the God who is beyond all words or images. Only secondarily does "believing" have to do with the doctrines and formulations of the Church.

We can get at the point of your question if we notice the ambiguity of the English word "believe," which we inevitably use when we want the verb that corresponds to the noun "faith." "Believe" can, of course, mean "to have firm faith, especially religious faith." But it can also mean "to accept something as true or real; to suppose, have an opinion, or think." (American Heritage Dictionary, 3rd ed.)

If by "believing" we mean accepting as true a series of propositions about God and "the things of God," then there is certainly room for serious intellectual work. All human formulations of divine truth are limited and relative to the cultural situation in which they were devised. To penetrate their deep meaning and to re-state it for a new cultural situation is the never-ending work of theology as an intellectual discipline.

Believers have a right to raise questions about Church doctrine, in order to come to a deeper and more correct understanding of God's truth. St. Anselm's concept of theology as "faith seeking understanding" (*fides quaerens intellectum*) is still valid, nearly a thousand years after he coined the phrase.

There is also the right and obligation to examine critically any account of the Christian faith which demands total adherence. From the earliest days of the Christian movement, there were divergent and competing interpretations of the gospel, so that it was necessary to discriminate and judge.

> *"Beloved, do not believe every spirit, but test the spirits to see whether they are from God; for many false prophets have gone out into the world." (1 Jn 4:1) "Do not quench the Spirit. Do not despise the words of prophets, but test everything; hold fast what is good, abstain from every form of evil." (1 Thess 5:19-22)*

Faithfulness to God and to the good news of Jesus Christ appears to demand that we be discriminating and discerning in what we accept as binding. This cannot happen without allowing room for questioning and ongoing theological dialogue and argument. The history of the Church's dogmatic tradition bears ample witness to this.

With regard to the many and varied styles of theological thinking, preaching and praying which one may encounter among Christians today, there is certainly need for critical appraisal and for discernment of the Spirit of God. Not everyone who urges us to accept his or her understanding of the gospel can automatically claim our whole-hearted assent.

But what about the primary meaning of "believing"— entrusting our very selves to God? Is there any room here for doubt, questioning, or intellectual activity?

We must recognize that, although we are called to a total trust in God, the degree of our trust (our faith) can vary greatly from hour to hour and day to day. It is a struggle sometimes to believe in God, because of the nature of our life experiences. Hesitation between belief and unbelief (in the primary sense) is sometimes our unavoidable condition.

To suppress all questions or doubts is to become a fanatic, who refuses to consider any criticism or objections. On the other hand, we can never completely rationalize the choice to believe in God. When all is said and done, it is a matter of the whole person, not just the intellect.

Jesus' urgent exhortation *"Do not fear. Only believe!"* (Mk 5:36) remains valid as the demand for a total surrender to God in trust, hope, and love. Despite our hesitations and inconsistencies, we must always respond to this as fully as we know how. We can perhaps find comfort in the words of the desperate father seeking help for his son: *"I believe; help my unbelief!"* (Mk 9:24)

Faithfully,

The Theologian

# Who and What is God?

Dear Theologian,

Who is God? What is God?

Seeking Wisdom

Dear Seeker,

You don't waste words, do you? These are questions that can never be answered adequately. But it is helpful to have them posed so simply and directly—almost as a child might ask them.

When confronted so directly and inescapably, the believer might well feel at a loss to answer. How can one put into words what is infinitely greater than the human mind? But we try. Since you have asked a theologian (not a mystic or a poet), you are going to get somewhat philosophical, rational answers. But there are other ways of responding to your questions—in sacred music, inspired songs, works of art, poems, and perhaps most convincingly, in the lives of holy men and women.

All speaking about God ought to be done with great humility, modesty and reverence. But this is not always the case. We Church people use the word "God" so often and so familiarly that we are in some danger of becoming glib and superficial in our "God-talk." We can lose the sense of awesome Mystery that must always accompany any serious speech about God.

We sense this Mystery at certain moments of heightened awareness. Peter Gomes speaks of "those close encounters of the transcendent kind that suggest relationships beyond the power of our experience to reckon, but which we know in some fundamental way to be true."[2] Most of us have had moments like that, when we were thrilled, shocked, or awed by an experience that drew us beyond the merely rational—the splendor of a sunset, the grandeur of mountains, the birth of a child, a Beethoven symphony. The list could be prolonged.

But WHAT is God? An old axiom says, "God is always greater" (*Deus semper major*)—that is, greater than anything we can imagine, conceive, or express. God cannot be put into a category of things,

2    Peter Gomes, *The Good Book: Reading the Bible with Mind and Heart* (New York: William Morrow & Company, 1996), p. 214.

because God is not one thing among many. God is the "ground of being" for all that is. So we are unable to answer in any satisfactory way the question, "What is God?" None of our answers to the what-question can possibly fit God.

Nevertheless, we have many "names" for God. The Bible is full of them (rock, fortress, shade from the heat, living water, blazing fire, shield, mother, father, etc.). These images function as metaphors, trying to say indirectly and poetically what cannot be said literally and directly. No one of these metaphors is adequate to the reality toward which they point. That's why there are so many of them. They are suggestive, but cannot be taken literally, and we cannot know to what extent each of them really "fits." It's as if the human mind is continually groping after more ways of referring to the nameless and unspeakable Mystery that underlies and fills all things.

WHO is God? This question seems to presuppose that God is personal. "Who" is a word that directs us toward a reality that we could properly address with the word "Thou" ("You"). And Christian believers do dare to address God with this personal pronoun. In fact, they even go further, following the teaching and example of Jesus, and dare to say "Father!"

But we are not to imagine God as a limited person in the way that each human being is. This would be the same kind of mistake as taking literally one of the "names" or metaphors for God. "God is always greater." Still and all, if one asks "Who is God?" one is looking for a reality that is at least not "sub-personal," though it may be "trans-personal."

The "who-ness" of God is discovered only by relating to God personally in prayer. When we try to speak to God, it feels right to say "Thou" or "You." In the attitude of praying, we enter into a personal relationship with "someone," not "some thing."

On the other hand, when we try to speak *about* God in personal terms, we fumble and fall into paradoxical language. We are embarrassed by the need to refer to God, then, as either "Him" or "Her," even though we don't really think that gender is relevant in speaking about God. Our little third-person pronouns are rightly felt to be utterly inadequate when we use them to refer to the One whom we know authentically only in an "I-Thou" relationship.

Whether, then, we try to say "Who" God is or "What" God is, we are left finally in reverent silence, to feel the unutterable Mystery. This is a good and blessed point to reach. But we human beings are reluctant to stay very long in that state of unknowing and wonder.

Although I may not have answered your questions in a satisfactory way, I hope that these reflections may help you to continue to live with those questions.

Faithfully,

The Theologian

# God and the Devil

Dear Theologian,

If God is the Creator of all that is, where did the Devil come from? Was the Devil created by God? But that would make God the author of evil! Putting the question another way: Isn't everything that is created by God *"very good"* (Gen 1:31)? Then where does evil come from? How is evil even possible?

Puzzling Over Good and Evil

Dear Puzzling,

Christian tradition considers the Devil to be a "fallen Angel," that is, a spiritual being that was created by God but refused to subject his will to God's will. As created, the Angel was "good," just as all things created by God are good. But this Angel used his freedom to reject God and to choose alienation and misery. He thus became "evil" himself, and a principle of evil that seeks to draw others into sin.

It's important to note here that authentic Christian faith does not consider the Devil to be an equal of God. It's not as if there were two equal principles—one good and one evil—endlessly battling each other. This kind of dualism is really alien to the Christian understanding that God is the Creator of all things.

But we're still left with the puzzle that you have named. If what God creates is good, how can it "go bad?" Where does evil come from? In fact, as you put it, how is evil even possible?

Before tackling this, let's make a distinction between "physical evil" and "moral evil." Earthquakes, floods and diseases are examples of physical evil (for the human beings affected by them). Many thinkers have struggled to reconcile such events with the belief that God's created world is "very good." From our limited point of view, it often doesn't seem that way.

I want to limit this discussion to "moral evil"—that is, the malicious choice by a free, rational creature to do what is harmful to self and others. History is replete with examples of this, both great and small. We might think spontaneously of the Nazis' cold-blooded carrying-out of genocide against the Jews. But there are other examples from more recent years in places such as Cambodia, Bosnia, Kosovo, and Rwanda. Moral evil on such a scale staggers and sickens the human heart.

There are also the smaller, less public instances of moral evil that occur constantly on all sides—causing great harm and suffering. We hear about them every day in the news media. And then there is the moral evil in ourselves that, if we are honest, we must discover and repent of.

So, although we believe in God as the totally good Creator of all that is, we have to recognize that the world God creates is actually shot through with moral evil. How can we account for this state of affairs? Why would God create a world where such things are possible?

At this point, we come up against the sheer paradox of "created freedom." In creating, God really "lets" things exist on their own, apart from God. And some of the beings that God "lets be" have the freedom to choose either good or evil.

But why would God create a world in which some of God's creatures can and do choose moral evil? The answer has to be sought in some understanding of why freedom is apparently so important to God. What God ultimately intends, we believe, is the free response of God's creatures to the Love which creates and redeems them. And it is only beings who can choose either good or evil who can freely choose the good.

So, we might say that God takes a great risk in creating—the risk that the creatures will choose evil and "nothingness" rather than the fullness of being that God intends for them.

But this is not the whole story. The Love which "lets" the creatures exist as free beings, capable of choosing evil, does more than create. As Christian faith affirms, this Love also enters personally into the created order to redeem and save the creatures who would otherwise be "lost."

In Christ's incarnation, death and resurrection, evil is overcome by good. And those who participate now in his suffering look forward to a future in which they will participate in his glory. In the meantime, they are called to embody his saving love, which alone can counter the moral evil in the world.

To return to your original question, we might say this: God did not create "a Devil." God created a spiritual being (an "Angel") whose very existence sprang from the unqualified goodness of God. The Angel who chose evil became "the Devil" by his own free choice.

Following the same line of thought, God does not create "morally evil beings." God creates beings that are fundamentally good insofar as they spring from God's utter goodness. But the creatures endowed with freedom can and do choose moral evil. Even so, they do not become totally evil.

Furthermore, Christian faith recognizes in Christ the permanent, unswerving intention of God to forgive and reconcile all who will renounce evil and chose good once again. No one, in this view, is absolutely "lost" except by stubbornly choosing to remain in that condition. The Christian theologian Origen (third century) speculated that even the Devil would ultimately "turn back" to God and be reconciled with the Love that holds him in being.

Moral evil is an anomaly in the God-created world, to be sure. In principle, it "should not be." But in actuality, it appears to have been part of the human scene from the very beginnings of human life. Nevertheless, the faithful and merciful Love that is at the heart of things has also been present from the beginning. That Love has become flesh in Christ, and has been victorious over sin and death.

It is for us to bear witness to Him in the way we encounter the moral evil in the world. We are to do our best to live by St. Paul's words to the believers in Rome: *"Do not be overcome by evil, but overcome evil with good."* (Rom 12:21).

Faithfully,

The Theologian

# Revelation

Dear Theologian,

My question is about the meaning of the word "revelation." It occurred in one of the Sunday readings just recently: *"The mystery was made known to me by revelation.... In former generations this mystery was not made known to humankind, as it has now been revealed to his holy apostles and prophets by the Spirit."* (Eph 3) Just what does the term "revelation" mean? Is it important for our life of faith?

Not Yet Enlightened

Dear Not Yet,

The English word "revelation" translates the Greek word APOKÁLYPSIS, which literally means the "uncovering" or "disclosing" (of something that had been hidden). This noun or its verb form occurs in a number of places in the New Testament. It always has to do with the disclosure or unveiling of the divine or of some aspect of the divine will.

On the one hand, God is absolute Mystery, utterly beyond human comprehension. On the other hand, God graciously comes near to us in and through our experience of the created world. Christians as well as Jews believe that God takes the initiative in establishing a relationship with human beings. In this view, it is not really a matter of our "search" for God. Rather, in the words of the great Jewish scholar Rabbi Abraham Heschel, it is "God in search of man."

In the revelatory experience, writes Anglican theologian John Macquarrie, "it is as if the holy 'breaks in' and the movement is from beyond man toward man."[3] What one comes to know through the revelatory experience, therefore, has a gift-character. He goes on to note that almost anything in the world can be an occasion for revelation—natural phenomena, for example, or historical events and personal relationships.

---

3    John Macquarrie, Principles of Christian Theology, 2nd ed. (New York: Charles Scribner's Sons, 1977), p. 7.

But there is a paradox involved in speaking of revelation. For God, though in some sense "disclosed" through the revelation, still remains utterly "hidden" and beyond human grasp.

In the Hebrew Scriptures, it is said that no one can "see the face of God" without being destroyed (Ex 33:20). The "glory" of God rests upon some created reality, and—as it were—shines through it. (For example, *"The glory of the Lord settled on Mount Sinai... like a devouring fire on the top of the mountain in the sight of the people of Israel."* Ex 24:16-17) One sees the "glory," but cannot see God directly.

Consider the story of the "transfiguration" of Jesus (Lk 9:28-36). The glory of God streams out through Jesus, changing his appearance into dazzling light. Then the cloud (symbol of God's hiddenness) covers them, and they feel a holy fear. What the voice (of God) says to them is significant: *"This is my beloved Son. Listen to him."* When they look up they see "only Jesus"—that is, only the familiar, very human reality of their teacher and friend. He is the one to whom they are to pay close attention, in order to know the hidden God.

The human recipient of God's self-disclosure receives the gift through his or her own imagination and culture. This is especially true of the one who receives what we might call an "original" or "originating" revelation (such as Moses, for example). Macquarrie uses the term "primordial revelation" for this kind of revelatory event, since it becomes foundational for all further revelatory experiences in the cultural tradition that stems from it.

The human expression of the primordial revelation, handed down through Scripture and tradition, then becomes for other human beings an occasion for their own revelatory experiences. In their own way, they "repeat" and experience afresh what was once given. This way of looking at the matter helps to understand how Scripture functions in the faith-life of present-day Christian believers.

A revelatory experience is "given" graciously by God. It is the work of the Holy Spirit interacting with human consciousness. On the other hand, the openness or receptivity of the human person is also a factor in what is experienced.

For us Christians, the greatest revelation is Christ himself. Brother and Lord, Jesus abides forever as completely human and completely divine. To recognize him as the Christ is always a revelatory experience, whenever and as often as it occurs. When the disciple Simon confessed Jesus as the Christ, Jesus replied: *"Blessed are you, Simon son of Jonah! For flesh and blood has not <u>revealed</u> this to you, but my Father in heaven."* (Mt 16:17, emphasis added). And the apostle Paul said of his own discovery of the Lord: *"I received [the gospel] through a <u>revelation</u> of Jesus Christ... God, who had set me apart before I was born and called me through his grace, was pleased to <u>reveal</u> his Son to me."* (Gal 1:12,15, emphasis added).

Faithfully,

The Theologian

# Section 2: The Mystery of Christ

What is said about Jesus as the Christ in the following group of essays springs from the author's life-long involvement with this great Mystery as a member of the Church catholic—for many years in the Roman communion and then for over three decades in the Anglican communion.

The intention, in each of these responses, is to express faithfully what the Church has come to believe and to teach. There is no attempt to "work out" an original Christology. On the other hand, the author does have his own typical way of formulating the Church's faith and tends to return repeatedly to certain key themes.

# Baptism of Jesus

Dear Theologian,

Why was Jesus baptized? Didn't John's baptism signify repentance for sins? Yet we say that Jesus was sinless. So what could baptism by John mean for Jesus?

Interested

Dear Interested,

The story of Jesus' baptism by John derives from an actual historical event, scholars argue, precisely because the tradition was preserved even though it was awkward for Christian believers to deal with. Jesus' submission to John's baptism did not seem fitting, somehow. In Matthew's version, the Baptist first objects that he should be baptized by Jesus, not Jesus by him. And in Luke, the story of Jesus' baptism does not actually name John as the agent.

In the gospel accounts, there is no indication that Jesus is expressing repentance for his own sins when he goes down under the water. But one might think that he is entering into the larger meaning of John's baptism: openness to the coming of the Kingdom of God. And some have interpreted his action as an expression of his solidarity with sinful mankind.

Although the gospel tradition provides no clarity about why Jesus submitted to the baptism or what this could have meant to him, it leaves no doubt about the meaning of Jesus' revelatory experience when he comes up out of the water. This is the culminating event, as presented in all three synoptic gospels (Matthew, Mark and Luke). It expresses powerfully the unique relationship of Jesus to God.

Jesus sees the heavens "opened" and the Holy Spirit descending upon him in the form of a dove. And he hears the voice of God: *"You are my Son, the Beloved; with you I am well pleased."* (Mk 1:10-11; Mt 3:16-17; Lk 3:21-22)

It is somewhat unclear whether it is only Jesus that experiences the vision and hears the voice of God, or whether others also see and hear. Luke's version adds the detail that, after his baptism, Jesus was praying. This seems to indicate that the experience was unique to him.

In all three accounts, the baptismal experience precedes any public ministry of Jesus. It is a moment of God-given certainty about his identity as "Son" and as "Beloved," and therefore also a decisive moment of awareness of his unique vocation and task.

What follows upon this experience is the irresistible impulse to go away into solitude, to be alone with God and with this new self-knowledge.

The time in the wilderness is, then, a period of struggling to interpret rightly the revelation of his unique status and call. He is tempted to false understandings of it, but resolutely chooses the stance of humility and utter obedience to God. Only then is he ready to begin his public ministry, in the course of which he will speak with authority and certainty the message of the Kingdom of God, and will give dramatic signs of the coming of that Kingdom in his exorcisms and healings.

Rightly understood, the story of Jesus' baptism and the revelation which followed upon it is full of meaning for Christian believers. It may be regarded as one of the "mysteries" of Christ's life (events with an infinite dimension of depth, to be entered into only through meditation and prayer). It is the mystery of his relationship to God as Father and his profound experience of being "Son."

This is a mystery in which we somehow share. Upon each of us, too, the Holy Spirit descends with transforming power. To each of us, too, God says, "You are my son / my daughter; with you I am well pleased."

St. Paul bears witness to this sharing of Christians in the "sonship" of Jesus:

> "When the fullness of time had come, God sent his Son, born of a woman, born under the law, so that we might receive adoption as sons [and daughters]. And because you are sons [and daughters], God has sent the Spirit of his Son into your hearts, crying 'Abba! Father!'" (Gal 4:4-6)

*"All who are led by the Spirit of God are sons [and daughters] of God. For you did not receive a spirit of slavery to fall back into fear, but you have received a spirit of adoption by which we cry 'Abba! Father!'"* (Rom 8:14-15)

We enter into our inheritance as sons and daughters of God when we are baptized into Jesus and accept him as our Savior and Lord. As his adopted brothers and sisters, we are able to relate to the unimaginable Mystery of God with utter trust and confidence.

*"...in Christ Jesus our Lord ... we have access to God in boldness and confidence through faith in him."* (Eph 3:12) In the Eucharistic liturgy, the presider says, "as our Savior Christ has taught us, we are <u>bold</u> to say, 'Our Father." [4]

There is another perspective on Jesus' baptism which is also basic to our Christian identity as sharing in his mystery. One might view his going down into the water as his submission to the Father's will and his dedication to the unique vocation he was given. Ultimately, of course, that would involve his being rejected, undergoing great suffering, and dying a shameful death.

He himself uses the metaphor of baptism to refer to the ordeal which lies before him. *"I have a baptism with which to be baptized, and what stress I am under until it is completed!"* (Lk 12:50)

Our own sacramental baptism signifies our identification with Christ in the Paschal Mystery of his death and resurrection (Rom 6:3-11). This means that we, like Jesus, dedicate ourselves to the vocation God gives us and that we, like him, submit humbly to the will of the Father for our lives. In a way, our baptism signifies our taking upon ourselves our own unique sharing in the mystery of God's redeeming love for the world.

What Jesus says to James and John, he also says to each of us who have been given a share in the meaning of his baptism: *"The cup that I drink you will drink; and with the baptism with which I am baptized, you will be baptized."* (Mk 10:39) Knowing what this implies, we might be afraid, but we trust utterly in the Father, as Jesus did. *"If we have been united with him in a death like his, we will certainly be united with him in a resurrection like his."* (Rom 6:5)

Faithfully,

The Theologian

---

4    BCP, p. 363, emphasis added.

# Incarnation

Dear Theologian,

In the Nicene creed that we recite every Sunday, there are a lot of things that I don't really understand. My question right now is about just one phrase: "...he ['the only Son of God'] became incarnate from the Virgin Mary, and was made man." I have heard priests speak about the doctrine of the Incarnation, and I realize that it is central to our Christian faith. But what is it really saying?

Seeking Understanding

Dear Seeker,

To put it very simply, the doctrine of the Incarnation is saying that God has become man. This is an understanding of the mystery of Jesus that emerged out of the spiritual experience of the first believers, but had to be clarified and carefully defined through several centuries of controversy within the Church.

This doctrine touches directly and deeply upon every Christian believer's relationship with God. For the Christian way of knowing, loving and being united with God is the way of the Incarnate One, who is the Crucified and Risen One.

People ask at times, "How do I relate to Jesus?" or "How is Jesus involved in my relationship with God?" The doctrine of the Incarnation is crucial for answering such questions in a way that is faithful to the living tradition of the Church.

It is difficult, though, for Christians to stay with the paradox that is being affirmed when we say that, in Jesus, God has become man. It is all too easy to slide off onto one side or the other—either regarding Jesus simply as God, or regarding him merely as a human being.

The tendency to regard Christ only as human is common today, particularly among people who are confused and uncertain about the meaning of his "divinity." This is true not only of those outside the Church, but also of many within who struggle to make sense of their Christian faith. They can relate to him as teacher and holy man, or as model of how to be authentically human. They hesitate at being asked to address him as divine.

On the other hand, those who simply equate Jesus with God do not give full weight to his humanity. Such a view attributes to Jesus a consciousness identical with that of God. He knows all things, including the future suffering that awaits him.

In affirming the doctrine of the Incarnation, we are not saying that God pretended to be human. We are saying that God "became" a complete human being, with a human soul and consciousness, a particular culture and language, and a particular history. We are saying that the entire life process of this one human being, from conception until death, is God's definitive self-expression. In and through and *as* Jesus, God speaks the eternal Word.

Putting it that way heightens the paradox almost to the breaking point, and we can see why many people "stumble" over the scandal of Christ.

But there is more. Christian faith regards Christ not only as God's Word to the human race, but also as the perfect human response to God. Jesus, in his living and finally in his dying, gives to God the perfect praise, love and obedient surrender that constitute a human person's perfect union with God. In his resurrection, then, he becomes 'the new Adam,' the archetype and principle of a new way of being human that is now available to all other human beings.

This faith grounds the hope with which we Christians live out our journey. In proclaiming the "Paschal Mystery," we believe that Christ has, so to speak, taken our humanity through the unimaginable passage of death into the Presence. We hope to be so aligned with and identified with Christ that we will also be brought with him into that same blessed Presence through our own passage of death.

At the end of this reflection, we do well to remember that the Incarnation is the absolute, incomprehensible mystery at the center of Christian faith in God. Although the human mind can never penetrate it with rational understanding, it is the inescapable reality for all those who confess Jesus as Lord.

Faithfully,

The Theologian

# Paschal Mystery

Dear Theologian,

Our liturgy of the Easter Vigil speaks of "the Paschal Mystery."[5] I've heard this phrase in sermons from time to time, but have never really understood just what it means. Is this important for living the Christian faith? If it is, how can I understand it?

A Believer Needing an Explanation

Dear Believer,

Let's begin with the word "mystery." Although this word comes up fairly often in Christian discourse, it is seldom explained. Its ordinary meaning in every-day English is: "Something that is not fully understood or that baffles or eludes the understanding." In this sense one might speak of a "murder mystery" or say, "It's a mystery to me." This kind of mystery can, in principle, be "solved." We can come to a full understanding of the matter..

In Christian theology, the word "mystery" is used differently. The ordinary meaning is still there, but a new dimension is added. "Mystery" now means a reality which is too great for the human mind ever to understand fully. Some understanding is possible, of course. Otherwise, nothing whatever could be said about it. But full and complete understanding is impossible, since it exceeds absolutely the human mind's capacity.

In this sense, God is the Mystery. Moreover, things which are closely associated with God are also "mysteries," insofar as the God-dimension of them remains forever beyond human comprehension. This applies, above all, to Jesus Christ and to the events of his life. It applies, in a secondary way, to the Church, the Sacred Scriptures, the sacraments, etc. The doctrinal truths of Christian faith are also called "mysteries" in this sense.

What about the adjective "Paschal"? It can refer to either the Jewish Passover or the Christian Easter.

What "Passover" meant (and still means) to Jews is the wonderful act of God that set them free from slavery in Egypt. The angel of death

---

5      BCP, p. 292.

sent by God to destroy the first-born of the Egyptians "passed over" the homes of the Hebrews because their doorposts had been sprinkled with the blood of the sacrificed lamb. (Ex 12:21-23) Shaken by this mighty sign of God's power, the Egyptians let the Hebrews go forth into freedom (the "Exodus" from slavery).

Jesus was crucified by the Romans at the time of the annual Passover celebration in Jerusalem. According to John's Gospel, he died at the very time that the lambs were being sacrificed in the temple. So it came naturally for Christians to think of him in the image of the Passover lamb. His cruel death by public execution was understood in faith as the sacrifice by which all human beings were set free from slavery to sin. And his glorious resurrection was understood to be his victory over sin and death, a victory which all others were meant to share.

The "Paschal Mystery," therefore, means the death and resurrection of Christ, the event by which he himself "passed over" from this earthly human condition into the eternal joy of the Father. Christians identify with him by being baptized "into his death" and "rising up" from the baptismal waters into a new life in the power of the Holy Spirit. (Cf. Rom 6:3-4)

The Paschal Mystery is at the center of Christian faith. To be Christian is to belong to the Crucified and Risen One. This means that each of us lives out our life in close union and identification with him. The Paschal Mystery becomes our mystery as well. It is our passage through death into new life. And our ultimate hope is to be risen with Christ. As St. Paul put it, "... *if we have been united with him in a death like his, we will certainly be united with him in a resurrection like his... if we have died with Christ, we believe that we will also live with him.* " (Rom 6:5,8)

Faithfully,
The Theologian

# Reconciliation

Dear Theologian,

After seeing the Passion movie, I need to ask: Why did Jesus have to undergo such a horrible ordeal? And what does it mean to say that Jesus suffered and died for our sins?

Disturbed Moviegoer

Dear Moviegoer,

The Mel Gibson film is a graphic and relentless depiction of Jesus' suffering. For those of us who confess him as Lord and Christ, it may well be the occasion to reflect deeply on our own understanding of the Paschal Mystery.

The passion, death, and resurrection of Jesus is the very heart and center of our life of faith. It is what we remember and participate in every time we celebrate the Holy Eucharist. Yet it remains a mystery that we cannot penetrate with our rational mind.

The disciples of Jesus could not at first find any meaning in what happened to him at the end. Only in the light of his resurrection were they able—by searching the Hebrew scriptures—to interpret his suffering and death as something foretold by the prophets, and hence as part of God's eternal plan of salvation.

This is brought out simply and movingly in the Emmaus story in Luke's gospel (Lk 24:13-35). In that passage, the Stranger on the road (the risen Lord) says to the two disciples: *"How slow of heart [you are] to believe all that the prophets have declared! Was it not necessary that the Messiah should suffer these things and then enter into his glory?"*

"Was it not necessary?" Apparently it was, but how can we begin to understand this? If this terrible fate was, indeed, included in God's intention of "saving" mankind, how does it relate to our salvation?

In the New Testament as a whole, Christ's death on the cross is regarded as the focal point of God's action of "reconciling" sinful humanity to Himself. Paul says,

> *"... while we were enemies, we were reconciled to God by the death of his Son."* (Rom 5:10) And again, *" God ... reconciled us to himself through Christ, and has given us the ministry of reconciliation; that is, in Christ God was reconciling the world to himself, not counting their trespasses against them, and entrusting the message of reconciliation to us."* (2 Cor 5:18-19)

Like most, if not all, theological words, "reconciliation" has its literal meaning in the world of ordinary human experience. What does it mean to reconcile, in ordinary usage? It means to bring back into a proper relationship persons or things which have become incompatible. When the word is used theologically, it refers to the mystery of how the estrangement of human beings from God is overcome.

It presupposes the negative state of estrangement or "alienation"—being separated or cut off from that to which one belongs. A vivid image of this is given in the story of the first human beings, after the Fall, hiding from God among the trees. (Gen 3) They were afraid and ashamed, unwilling to interact with the One to whom they belonged.

Christian faith affirms that the alienation of human beings from God has been overcome, in principle, by the life, death and resurrection of Jesus of Nazareth. But how are we to understand this? What difference did/does Christ make? What is it about his existence in our world that re-unites us with the God from whom we are alienated?

In the Hebrew scriptures, God repeatedly urges the people of Israel to "turn," that is, turn back toward the God of the covenant. (Isa 31:6, 45:22; Jer 15:19; Ezek 18:32) God also complains about the unsteadiness and stubborn refusal of his people. (Hos 6:4; Jer 5:3) The estrangement that keeps happening is caused by the people's lack of a consistent response to God's steady love.

This is important for how we interpret the "reconciling" quality of Jesus' life, death, and resurrection. There is no obstacle to reconciliation from God's side, but only from the side of sinful and alienated human beings. The question then becomes, How does Christ change the human side of the relationship?

Is it only his suffering and death that matter? But his death is unintelligible when isolated from his ministry and teaching. It is surely wrong to think that Jesus came only to suffer and die. It is wrong to think that it was only his torture and violent death—accepted willingly—that redeemed mankind. Surely it was his entire existence as "child" or "servant" of God that mattered.

Christ himself was "turned" utterly "toward God" in his living and finally in his dying. The Passion was the supreme test of Jesus' obedience to the Father. It was the culmination of a life that belonged wholly to God.

> *"He emptied himself, taking the form of a slave, being born in human likeness. And being found in human form, he humbled himself and became obedient to the point of death— even death on a cross."* (Phil 2:7-8) *"Although he was a Son, he learned obedience through what he suffered."* (Heb 5:8)

Jesus' suffering and death was the outcome of a life lived in utter faithfulness to God. His offer of forgiveness and reconciliation with God was misunderstood and rejected by human beings. This is poignantly expressed in Jesus' lament over Jerusalem: *"How often have I desired to gather your children together as a hen gathers her brood under her wings, and you were not willing!"* (Lk 13:34)

Why did Christ suffer? We could say that we human beings— represented by some Jewish leaders and the Roman governor at the time—rejected the revelation of God that was presented to us in the person, ministry and teaching of Jesus of Nazareth. If we regard Jesus as the divine Love incarnate, then our human sinfulness rejected that Love and, indeed, crucified it.

If that were the end of the story, we might not think of reconciliation between human beings and God. But the Cross is not the final word. The Resurrection of Jesus is the triumphant re-affirmation of divine Love, despite the worst that human beings can do.

This is suffering Love, which overcomes evil with good. It is finally victorious by "absorbing" all the malice of human beings and repaying it with infinite mercy. The first word that the risen Lord speaks to the disciples who had abandoned him is *"Shalom! Peace!"* (Jn 20:19) This is the word which he continues to speak to each of us, whenever we turn again toward him.

In Christ,

The Theologian

# Resurrection

Dear Theologian,

As a member of the Church, I affirm each Sunday my faith that Jesus is risen from the dead. But what does this mean for my own relationship with God?

Pilgrim

Dear Pilgrim,

A way into this question might be to ask yourself how seriously you take Jesus' death. Do you think of it as a momentary episode in a progression toward glory? Or do you think of it as the real end of his human pilgrimage?

If—as we believe—he is risen, that doesn't mean that he has simply "come back to life," that is, to the kind of life he had before. He has gone beyond the kind of life that we know anything about.

Yet it is still he, and he is still in relation to the world of time and change—but in a totally new way. We say that he is victorious, that he "reigns." He relates to the world in the utter sovereignty and freedom of God.

But what about us who are not yet risen, who are still in the process of living out our own human pilgrimage? What does it mean for us to believe that Jesus is risen? How does this faith affect our own way of believing in God?

The reality that we know anything about first-hand is process, change, becoming, growing and eventually declining, being subject to pain and injury, being subject finally to the loss of life itself.

What is it like, then, for us Christians to believe in God while accepting our transience and impermanence? Can we hope for anything more than what we know here and now in our mortal existence?

To believe that Jesus is risen is to believe that ultimate reality is totally affirming of human existence. The "Alleluia" that we sing expresses our certainty that God is good beyond all expectation. It is right to hope for a destiny that transcends the mortal life that we know.

To believe that Jesus is risen is to believe in *"the God ... who gives life to the dead and calls into existence the things that do not exist.*" (Rom 4:17) It is to entrust ourselves ever more completely to this Mystery that creates and re-creates, and that makes justice and truth finally to triumph. We dare to do this, even though we walk in the valley of the shadow of death. For death, seemingly all-powerful over all things human, is not the last word about our condition.

This Easter faith empowers us to go through all things without despairing, to expend our energy and time for the good of the human family, even though all is threatened by death, to encounter evil and suffer from it without losing heart, to be joyful in the midst of loss. *"... as dying, and see—we are alive; ...as sorrowful, yet always rejoicing; as poor, yet making many rich; as having nothing, and yet possessing everything."* (2 Cor 6:9-10)

This also has an important application to the corporate life of the Church. Our congregations are imperfect and not completely faithful, all too subject to sin and death. If there is life in us, life for the world, it does not come from us. The fruits of the Spirit are signs of the risen life of the Lord as he lives in each of us and in all of us together. By these things people may recognize that we belong to him: *"...love, joy, peace, patience, kindness, goodness, faithfulness, gentleness, and self-control."* (Gal 5:22-23)

If the Church's season of "Eastertide" means more than the reality of spring, it means that we live in a time of victory anticipated because assured. Jesus is the first to be risen, but all those who belong to him will also rise from the dead.

> *"...Christ has been raised from the dead, the first fruits of those who have died. For since death came through a human being, the resurrection of the dead has also come through a human being; for as all die in Adam, so all will be made alive in Christ. But each in his own order: Christ the first fruits, then at his coming those who belong to Christ."* (1 Cor 15:20-23)

Our ultimate hope, then, is to be risen with Christ. *"... if we have been united with him in a death like his, we will certainly be united with him in a resurrection like his... if we have died with Christ, we believe that we will also live with him."* (Rom 6:5,8)

The solemn gladness of Easter does not, of course, exempt us from our condition of temporality and mortality. The Lord is risen indeed, but we are not yet risen. We are still "on the way," living out the days and nights of our pilgrimage.

But when we live in the attitude of Easter faith, we have a hope to share with all other pilgrims. We know a secret that lies at the heart of things, and we have a reason for exultant joy and faithful service.

In Christ,

The Theologian

# Through Christ

Dear Theologian,

Why do the liturgical prayers of the Church typically end with the words "through Jesus Christ our Lord"? What does this mean, anyway?

Faithful Church-goer

Dear Church-goer,

Your question points to the fundamental dynamic of Christian faith life. It is only Christians who address God in this peculiar way. To ask why they do this is to be drawn more deeply into the mystery of Jesus the Christ. This is a matter of every-day spirituality for all believers, not merely a question of liturgical correctness.

From the very beginnings of Christianity, believers have had to consider how Jesus the Crucified and Risen One was involved in their relationship with God.

The Church's liturgical way of praying "*through* Jesus Christ our Lord" expresses clearly the mediating function of Christ. We find the same pattern in nearly every Collect prayer. It is expressed most powerfully in the climactic words of the Great Thanksgiving in the celebration of the Eucharist: "By him, and with him, and in him, in the unity of the Holy Spirit, all honor and glory is yours, Almighty Father, now and for ever. Amen."

This way of praying establishes the pattern not only for our "asking" but for our very existence in relationship to God.

Our faith in Jesus as "the Christ" or "the Lord" does not terminate in him; rather it leads us through and with him into his eternal relationship to the Father in the unity of the Spirit.

Jesus recognized as the Christ brings people to the Father, so that they become intimate sons and daughters of the living God. In this relationship of utter intimacy there is no place for fear or shame, as we cry out to God with the same word that Jesus used, *"Abba! Father!"* (Gal 4:6, Rom 8:15-16)

Notice the consequences of this truth for everyday faith-living. We have confident "access" (Eph 3:12) to the unspeakable mystery of God because we are baptized into a permanent union with Jesus our brother, a fellow human being who is like us in all things except sin, but whose humanity is united inseparably with the eternal Word.

It is by God's sheer graciousness that we have been brought into this "family relationship." When the celebrant of the Eucharist introduces the Lord's Prayer, we are reminded that it is an act of staggering audacity to address the eternal Mystery with the intimate family word, "Father." It is only because we have been made one with Jesus the Son that we dare to do this. "And now, as our Savior Christ has taught us, we are bold to say ... Our Father." [6]

All this is implied in the simple liturgical formula, "through Jesus Christ our Lord." To become aware of it is to enter more deeply into our day-to-day living of the great mystery of our baptism.

To let this influence our thinking may help to resolve some of the nagging uncertainties that sometimes trouble our minds. Instead of asking, "where is Jesus in my relationship with God," we may wind up asking, "where am I in that identification with Jesus which makes my relationship with God intimate and saving?"

Faithfully,
The Theologian

# Section 3: The Mystery of the Church

What is said about the Church in this group of essays reflects the author's faith and understanding as a Catholic Christian. The group begins with a question about the Holy Spirit, because belief in the Holy Spirit is foundational for the entire life of the Church and of its individual members.

There is, of course, no pretense of treating the vast subject matter of Ecclesiology. Only a few particular aspects of the meaning of Church are treated, in response to specific questions.

# Believing in the Holy Spirit

Dear Theologian,

Every Sunday, when we recite the Creed, I find myself saying, "We believe in the Holy Spirit..." What does it mean to believe in the Holy Spirit? Does it make any difference in the way I am to understand and live my Christian life?

Uninformed

Dear Uninformed,

In asking about the Holy Spirit, you are asking about God, and so any attempt to answer your question will involve the use of religious symbolism. This kind of symbolism, derived from Sacred Scripture, permeates our shared life of faith. When we appreciate its significance, it can draw us deeply into the Mystery that is too great for our conceptual and rational language. This is especially true when we try to think about the Holy Spirit.

In Scripture, fire is often associated with the awesome power and holiness of God. For example, Moses hides his face in reverence before the burning bush (Ex 3:1-6). Later, when he has brought the people of Israel to the sacred mountain in the desert, God's glory appears as a raging fire upon the mountain top (Ex 24:16-17).

The story of Pentecost in the New Testament takes the image of "the fire of God" to a different level of encounter and intimacy. There, the blazing energy of God is imagined as settling upon, filling and empowering each disciple in a way that is unique and personal. *"Divided tongues, as of fire, appeared among them, and a tongue rested on each of them. All of them were filled with the Holy Spirit ... "* (Acts 2:3-4)

Fire is not the only symbol of the Spirit in Scripture. Equally prominent and suggestive are the symbols wind and breath. In fact, there is a single Hebrew word, RUACH, that can be translated as either "spirit" or "wind" or "breath," depending on the context.

In the account of creation, in the very first book of the Bible, God's *ruach* is said to move or hover over the dark and formless waters of chaos. (Gen 1:2) This can be translated variously: *"The Spirit of God moved upon the face of the waters"* (KJV), *"... a wind from God swept over the face of the waters."* (NRSV).

The image of breath is found already in the second chapter of Genesis: *"...the LORD God formed man from the dust of the ground, and breathed into his nostrils the breath of life; and the man became a living being."* (Gen 2:7)

Both wind and breath occur again in the magnificent vision of the valley of dry bones in Ezekiel 37. The mighty wind/breath/spirit of God brings the dead to life, signifying God's intention to resurrect his people Israel from the grave and restore them in their own land.

The most vivid and moving use of the breath image occurs in the New Testament, when the risen Christ comes to his disciples, bringing them peace and imparting to them the Holy Spirit. Just as the first human being was created when God breathed his own Spirit into the "earth creature" (Gen 2:7), so now the disciples are created anew when Christ breathes his Spirit into them.

> *"Jesus said to them, 'Peace be with you. As the Father has sent me, so I send you.' When he had said this, he breathed on them and said to them, 'Receive the Holy Spirit.'"* (Jn 20:21-22)

Image and narrative draw us into the great Mystery and invite us to believe in it. In order, however, to unfold the implications of such belief, we also need at times the more prosaic and rational language of theologians. So let me quote now from the Catechism of the Book of Common Prayer.

"The Holy Spirit is the Third Person of the Trinity, God at work in the world and in the Church even now."[7] This very succinct formulation of the Church's teaching about the Holy Spirit needs to be developed and unfolded in order to appreciate its profound meaning.

When we say "We believe in the Holy Spirit," we are first and foremost making an act of faith in God. But "believing in" the Holy Spirit is not merely a matter of acknowledging the "reality" of God

---

7      BCP, p. 852.

(believing "that God is"). It is a matter of entrusting oneself to God in an attitude of surrender, obedience, and utter openness.

Furthermore, God the Holy Spirit, to whom we entrust ourselves, must be understood as being "at work in the world and in the Church even now." The Spirit is active, dynamic, creative—bringing into being what did not exist and raising the dead to life. (Rom 4:17)

Truly believing in the Holy Spirit, with heart and mind, makes all the difference in how you understand and live your life of Christian commitment.

First of all, it means that you see your very life of faith in Christ as made possible only by the presence and power of God the Holy Spirit within you. It is sheer gift, not your own achievement.

Believing in the mystery of the Holy Spirit involves the attitude of utter and unqualified dependence upon God in all your efforts and labors. This involves a profound humility and detachment with regard to the good works that you carry out. This runs counter to the tendency to glory in one's own achievements (what St. Paul calls "boasting"). In reality, all is gift.

When we are submissive to the Spirit, we put ego aside and let God act through us. Instead of asking God to help us do something that we intend, we simply ask God to take us, fill us, and use us for God's purposes. Being yielded to the Spirit also involves being taught, strengthened, encouraged, and filled at times to overflowing with the joy of God.

The action of the Spirit is, of course, by no means limited to the individual. To believe in God the Holy Spirit is to believe that God is creating and continually renewing a community in history which lives with the life of the risen Jesus, a community that transcends all boundaries of time, place, race, and culture, a community in which sinful people are forgiven, healed, and transformed.

In this Spirit-created communion, there are many different gifts and functions, but one shared life "in Christ." "...we, who are many, are one body in Christ, and individually we are members one of another. We have gifts that differ according to the grace given to us..." (Rom 12:5-6)

Believing in the Holy Spirit allows us to live with hope in the midst of troubles, confusion, and uncertainty. This is true not only for each individual person, but also for the social reality that is the Church. If we believe that God the Holy Spirit is actively present, "at work," both in our personal journeys and in the long pilgrimage of the Church through history, we have a reason for hope, even though the present situation may look very dark. It is God the Holy Spirit who creates, guides, re-creates and renews the Church in every generation.

Believing in the Holy Spirit also gives us hope for the larger world beyond the Church—because the Holy Spirit is God "at work" in the entire world, in every individual human person and in every community of persons. Wherever we recognize healing and reconciliation, we can rejoice in the presence of the Holy Spirit.

Believing in the Holy Spirit enables us to live with a confident, positive attitude. We need not be afraid of the future, for it is God's future. We need not cling to past customs and thought patterns, but can be open to the new. For it is characteristic of God the Creator Spirit to be always doing something new. *"Do not remember the former things, or consider the things of old. I am about to do a new thing; now it springs forth, do you not perceive it?"* (Isa 43:18-19)

It is a momentous confession of faith when we say, in the Creed, "We believe in the Holy Spirit." But it is perhaps only in personal prayer that each of us reaches the deepest realization of what this means.

In Christ,

The Theologian

# The One True Church

Dear Theologian:

My question concerns the nature of the Church. Once and for all, what is the "one true Church"? Roman Catholics say it is their Church, and Episcopalians are not part of it. Episcopalians say that their Church is a branch of the "one true Church." Other Churches say that their members are part of the "true Church" and so are other Christians. Who is right?

Tired of the Confusion

Dear Tired:

On this one, I can only give you my particular, limited perspective— as an historically and ecumenically oriented theologian living in the Anglican communion. I'll try to lay out some considerations that affect the answer, and then state my own view.

First, consider the biblical understanding of the Church. In the New Testament, the word we translate as "Church" (EKKLESÍA) is used mainly to refer to the community of Christian believers in one place. Secondarily, it is used to refer to the universal fellowship of all local congregations. It seems that each local community of faith exemplifies the mystery of the Church (the whole is present in each of its manifestations).

Moreover, the word has a profoundly spiritual meaning. It is variously understood as "the People of God," "the Creation of the Spirit," and "the Body of Christ." For a thorough treatment of these themes, Hans Küng's book *The Church* (first published in 1967) is still an excellent resource.

As the Christian movement grew and developed, there was need for institutional structures to assure continuity of doctrine and to keep the many local Churches in relationship with one another. An earlier form of local Church government by a group of "elders"

[PRESBYTEROI] was eventually replaced by the institution of a single, "monarchical" overseer, called a "bishop" [EPISKOPOS].

The bishop of each local Church was regarded as the chief teacher, whose communion with the many other bishops of other local Churches assured authentic doctrine, continuity with the beginnings, and union with the universal Church.

A further development came when certain cities were acknowledged as the main centers of Christianity—Antioch, Jerusalem, Alexandria, Rome, and eventually Constantinople. The bishops of those cities were called "patriarchs," and their higher authority came to be recognized by the other bishops in their respective regions. But these various groupings of local Churches understood themselves to be in communion with one another, and gradually the word "catholic" came to be used of the entire totality of local Churches. "Catholic" meant "universal" and "all-inclusive"—incorporating all regions of the world and all doctrines of the faith.

With the collapse of the Roman Empire in the West, the bishop of Rome began to take on ever greater importance as a unifying authority for those troubled regions.

The Church of Rome had, from early on, been especially honored and respected because of its links with Peter and Paul (who were both martyred there). But when the bishop of Rome (the patriarch of the West) came to assert authority over the entire "catholica," this claim was resisted by the patriarchs of the East. The cultural differences between East and West became ever greater.

In 1054 the split between the Church of the East and the Church of the West became final and definitive through mutual "excommunication." From that time on, each of the two regarded itself as the only true successor of the apostolic Church.

In the sixteenth century, the Reformation resulted in the further fragmentation of the Church of the West. The Church of Rome continued to regard itself as the only true Church, while the various "reformed" Churches saw themselves as authentic and faithful continuers of the apostolic faith.

Since then the splintering of the Western Church has continued, and it is probably here in the United States that the multiplicity of "denominations" is most evident. Hence your question.

In my view, the Church is always the creation of the Holy Spirit. It began with the flames of Pentecost, and continues to be re-created and renewed in every generation by the Creator Spirit.

Here is an image that helps me to think about this mystery of the Church being created ever anew by the Holy Spirit. Think of a force-field that arranges particles into a certain pattern whenever they come under its influence (like the lines of magnetic force revealed when a magnet is placed under a card with iron filings on it).

Wherever people are gathered in the name of Jesus, baptized into his death and resurrection, they are formed into a community created by the Holy Spirit. It has certain recognizable features—where the Gospel is truly preached, and the Sacraments faithfully celebrated, where the Sacred Scriptures are treasured and studied, where the fruits of the Holy Spirit are recognizable.

The Church, therefore, is never a purely spiritual and "invisible" reality. It is quite visible, historical, and recognizable. Christian faith has been and needs to be expressed in diverse cultural forms. Historical factors account for the great variety of manifestations of Church in the world today.

On the other hand, the present disunity of the many Churches is not to be regarded as "normal." In fact, it is a scandalous obstacle to the preaching of the Gospel among non-Christians. And it is manifestly contrary to the unifying intent of the Spirit.

What is to be done? Perhaps our best hope is to renew the ancient ideal of being in communion with one another, despite our diversity. Some of us imagine "a communion of communions."

Meanwhile, each Christian lives his or her faith "somewhere." I think it is right for every Christian believer to live his or her faith as fully as possible in the communion where he or she happens to be. But it is wrong, I think, to regard other communions as "not really Church," even though one is free to disagree with some of their ideas or practices.

But more than that: it is wrong for any Christian to accept as normal the present disunity of the one Church whose head is Christ. A faithful response to the Holy Spirit will lead each of our separated versions of Church to seek communion with the others.

In Christ,

The Theologian

# Communion of Saints

Dear Theologian,

What is meant by "the communion of saints"? Every time I recite the Apostles' Creed at Morning Prayer, I say that I believe in it, but I am vague about its meaning. Is this an important doctrine? And does it have any bearing on my own life of Christian faith?

Looking for Enlightenment

Dear Looking,

Let's start with the word "saints." We don't ordinarily apply this word to ourselves, since it seems to affirm a higher degree of holiness than we dare to claim. But it is a surprising fact that in the New Testament this word refers to all Christians. (Rom 1:7, 1 Cor 1:2)

This usage reflects the conviction that all those who belong to Christ through faith and baptism are called to be powerfully transformed by the Holy Spirit into the image of Christ. They are not necessarily morally better than other people, but they are involved in a process of being made holy, no matter how far they may be from reaching the goal (Phil 3:12-14).

What is meant, then, by the communion of saints? The word "communion" translates the Greek word KOINONÍA, which means fundamentally "a common sharing in" something. It can also be translated by the word "fellowship." For Christian faith, what the "saints" share in is Christ. So in the New Testament, KOINONÍA is the word used for the community of believers. What they have in common is the crucified and risen Lord who lives in them by the power of the Holy Spirit. *"God is faithful; by him you were called into the fellowship of his Son, Jesus Christ our Lord."* (1 Cor 1:9; see also Acts 2:41-42 and 1 Jn 1:3.)

This "fellowship" or "communion" involves the participants in a relationship of mutual love and solidarity.

*"As God's chosen ones, holy and beloved, clothe yourselves with compassion, kindness, humility, meekness, and patience. Bear with one another and, if anyone has a complaint against*

*another, forgive each other; just as the Lord has forgiven you, so you also must forgive. Above all, clothe yourselves with love, which binds everything together in perfect harmony."* (Col 3:12-14; see also Rom 12:9-10.)

This unique fellowship unites people of very different backgrounds, across all boundaries of race, class, or gender. It is not a matter of uniformity, but rather of "diversity in communion."

*"...in Christ Jesus you are all children of God through faith. As many of you as were baptized into Christ have clothed yourselves with Christ. There is no longer Jew or Greek, there is no longer slave or free, there is no longer male and female; for all of you are one in Christ Jesus."* (Gal 3:26-28; See also Col 3:11-12.)

Furthermore, as the Church has come to believe, this communion of people "in Christ" is not broken even by death. There is a spiritual unity of the living with all those who have gone before them in faith. The great fellowship extends beyond all boundaries of time or place, to include all those who have been or ever will be gathered into Christ.

Is the communion of saints an important doctrine of Christian faith? Rightly understood, it is central. St. Paul considered that the "mystery" of God's eternal purpose for mankind was revealed precisely in the joining together of Jews and Gentiles into one new community.

*"In former generations this mystery was not made known to humankind, as it has now been revealed to his holy apostles and prophets by the Spirit: that is, the Gentiles have become fellow heirs, members of the same body, and sharers in the promise in Christ Jesus through the gospel."* (Eph 3:5-6; see also Eph 2:11-22.)

Does the doctrine of the communion of saints have any bearing on your own life of Christian faith? Here are some considerations to ponder.

The life of faith that you live is really a participation in the communion of saints. To belong to Christ is to belong to his Body, the Church. If you let your living be illuminated by this truth, you will value highly your participation in the "fellowship" of the Church in various ways (liturgical worship, education, service, social interaction). You will not think of your personal spirituality as utterly private, but rather as a sharing in a great communal process of "formation" and indeed of "transformation" in Christ.

You will find strength and encouragement in the many witnesses who have lived the faith before your time. (Heb 12:1) You will also be strengthened by the good example of so many other people now living, in whom the mystery of Christ is "bodied forth."

And when you experience the death of people whom you have loved, your faith in the communion of saints will sustain you. The sharing in Christ which we have known together is not ended by death.

One final point: When we experience the joy and blessedness of sharing in the communion of saints, we desire to include others in that fellowship. We are motivated to be missionaries and apostles. This is well expressed in the First Letter of John:

> *"We declare to you what we have seen and heard, so that you also may have fellowship with us; and truly our fellowship is with the Father and with his Son Jesus Christ. We are writing these things so that our joy may be complete."*
> (1 Jn 1:3-4)

Faithfully,
The Theologian

# Apostolic

Dear Theologian,

What does the word "apostolic" mean when it occurs in the creed that we recite every Sunday? We say that "we believe in one holy catholic and apostolic Church." What is it about the Church that allows us to call it "apostolic," and does this quality have any importance for the ordinary member?

Curious

Dear Curious,

The term you are asking about is one of those "Church words" that we can hear and recite many times with little or no understanding of their meaning. But notice that it occurs in a profession of faith, in the third section of the Nicene creed which begins, "We believe in the Holy Spirit..." When we recite that familiar formula, therefore, we are affirming our faith in God the Holy Spirit as creator and sustainer of a Church which has the quality of being "apostolic."

The adjective "apostolic" itself does not occur anywhere in the Bible, but the "Church Fathers" use it constantly. It is first used by Ignatius of Antioch (1st-2nd century AD). Its original and most general meaning is "having a direct link with the apostles of Christ." From the second and third centuries the word "apostolic" also takes on the meaning of "like the apostles."

The key, therefore, to understanding the adjective "apostolic" is the meaning of the noun "apostle" (Greek APÓSTOLOS). This word is used in the New Testament, mainly by Luke (in his Gospel and in the Acts of the Apostles) and by Paul in his letters.

Its fundamental meaning (from the Greek verb APOSTÉLLEIN, "to send") is "one who is sent by another as messenger, emissary, representative, or ambassador." It seems that the term was used somewhat widely in the earliest years of the Christian movement for missionaries and messengers of the communities (cf. Phil 2:25), but later was limited (as in Luke) to "the Twelve," the inner circle of disciples chosen by Jesus himself.

St. Paul understood himself to be "apostle" in the sense of one commissioned and sent by the risen Christ for missionary preaching. Paul used the term frequently in this sense to refer to himself (e.g., the first verses of 1 and 2 Cor, Gal and Rom).

There are really two elements in this meaning of the New Testament term "apostle": (1) a witness of the risen Lord, one to whom the crucified Lord has revealed himself as living, and (2) one who has been commissioned by the Lord for missionary preaching.

The apostle is one sent by another (Christ) as his authorized ambassador. In himself he is nothing but a weak and frail human being who has his treasure in earthen vessels (2 Cor 4:7); apart from Christ he can do nothing (Jn 15:5).

But it is precisely in his full humanity that the apostle is chosen, called and sent out, to be the tool of God's grace (1 Cor 15:10; Rom 1:5). By preaching the gospel, the apostle arouses the response of faith and gathers together the fellowship of believers. By virtue of his message he is also authorized to found and to lead Churches and to exercise discipline in the Churches.

The Church is called "apostolic," therefore, first of all because it is founded on this ministry of "apostles." Without the witness and ministry of these first public witnesses authorized by Christ, without the ministry of Peter and the twelve, but also of James and all the other apostles down to the last, Paul, the Church could not exist.

The Church is called "apostolic" secondly because it continues to live in faithful continuity with the faith and teaching of the apostles. The preaching of the apostles, as it has come down to us in the writings of the New Testament, is the original, fundamental testimony to Jesus Christ, valid for all time. Later generations in the Church are dependent on the words, witness and ministry of the first "apostolic" generation.

How is all this relevant to the life of the individual Christian believer in the here and now? Here are some thoughts that might help.

By participating in the faith-life of an apostolic Church, one is joining oneself to a tradition that goes back to the first companions of Jesus. One is in touch with this great, ongoing history not as an outside observer but as an inside participant. If the Church itself is "apostolic," then each member must also be called to have the same quality.

Being apostolic—for each member of the Church—means being faithful to a blessed mystery that was enacted in time and space, at a particular moment and in a particular place. It is the mystery of Jesus the Crucified and Risen One.

Being apostolic involves a continual listening to the witness of the apostles, as preserved for us in the writings of the New Testament. Christian faith is not something to be invented anew by each generation, but a precious legacy for each generation to enter into.

Being apostolic, however, does not mean simply repeating the words and formulas of the New Testament or of early tradition. If the Church is to persist in its continuity with the beginnings, it must also find new and faithful ways of speaking and acting in each new cultural situation. Faithfulness must be combined with relevance.

On another level, being apostolic means, for the individual, sharing in the vocation of "being sent" by Christ to make his truth and his grace present and available to others. It means living and acting not merely in my own name, but in the name and power of the One who sends me. Weak and sinful as I am, I am continually being sent by Christ in his name to bring to others the good news of great joy and to lead them into the ways of peace.

Faithfully,
The Theologian

# Catholic

Dear Theologian,

What does the word "catholic" mean when it occurs in the creed that we recite every Sunday? We say that "we believe in one, holy, catholic and apostolic Church." And apparently we feel that we are included in this Church that we believe in. But "Catholic" is the word used to designate the Roman Catholic Church. In what sense can we apply that term to the Episcopal Church and the Anglican Communion?

Feeling Left Out

Dear Left Out,

The confusion arises because the English word "Catholic" (capitalized) has come to be equated, in common usage, with "Roman Catholic." But there is a more general meaning of the adjective "catholic," deriving from its origin in the Greek language. KATHOLIKÓS meant "universal" or "general," from the Greek expression KAT' HÓLOU ("by or according to the whole"). Hence, the first meaning of the English word "catholic" (not capitalized) is "comprehensive, universal," especially in the sense of "broad in sympathies, tastes, or interests."

A second meaning of the word, especially when it is capitalized, is "relating to or forming the Church universal." It can also mean "relating to or forming the ancient undivided Christian Church or a Church claiming historical continuity from it."

When the great schism between Eastern and Western Christianity became final in the eleventh century, both parts of the then divided Church understood themselves to be in continuity with the beginnings and, therefore, "catholic."

At the time of the Reformation, in the sixteenth century, the Western Church became fragmented. The portion of it which remained in communion with the Bishop of Rome continued to use the term "Catholic," but with the qualifying adjective "Roman." Moreover, it considered itself to be the only legitimate continuation of the ancient universal Church.

The Church of England, after separating from the authority of Rome, continued for some time to be and to think of itself as "Catholic." But the influence of the continental Reformers soon led to a more Protestant mentality and style of being Church. The tension between Catholic and Protestant forms of Christianity played a major part in the civil turmoil of England for a century or more, despite the settlement established under Queen Elizabeth. In the long run, however, the more Protestant style came to prevail.

The renewal of a more Catholic understanding of the Church of England began with the so-called Oxford Movement of the 19th century, associated with the names of Keble, Newman and Pusey. The influence of this movement gradually penetrated the Church of England as well as the American Episcopal Church and the emerging Anglican communion.

As a result, many Anglicans today affirm the "catholicity" of their communion. But what does this mean?

It means that Anglicans think of their Church as part of the great universal Church (not as a sectarian group maintaining itself in isolation). Moreover, they recognize and affirm that this one universal Church to which they belong is "catholic," as well as "holy" and "apostolic."

The term "catholic," as we have seen, has a long history as a designation of the Church. Although the term has come to be identified with the Roman form of Christian faith, it really has a rich meaning that can be honored and affirmed by other Christians, as well.

In general, it means "universal, all-embracing." This applies both to the extent of membership and to the fullness of doctrine that is affirmed. The one Church is for all human beings of every race, ethnic group, culture and language. And the faith of this one Church is articulated through a comprehensive and balanced set of doctrines that include all the essential aspects of the Christ mystery.

In the present state of things, however, we must recognize how tragically divided and fragmented the "one, holy, catholic and apostolic Church" actually is. What may we hope for?

In God's own time, we may hope for a greater spirit of true communion among the various Churches that bear the name of Jesus Christ. But the growing unity of spirit need not be expressed in the form of institutional uniformity and central control. The model could be that of "diversity in communion."

In Christ,

The Theologian

# Tradition

Dear Theologian,

What does the word "tradition" mean when it is used in a Church context? People often appeal to tradition in order to re-affirm what has been done in the Church for a long time, and sometimes to reject a new idea or practice. But what is tradition, where is it to be found, and how is it related to Scripture?

Baffled

Dear Baffled,

Let's begin with a standard dictionary definition of the word "tradition": 1. "the passing down of elements of a culture from generation to generation, especially by oral communication." 2. "a mode of thought or behavior followed by a people continuously from generation to generation; a custom or usage, or a set of such customs and usages viewed as a coherent body of precedents influencing the present."

Applying this concept to the life of the Church, we can say that "tradition means the continuous stream of explanation and elucidation of the primitive faith, illustrating the way in which Christianity has been presented and understood in past ages."[8] This might be correlated with the first meaning of the dictionary definition. But "tradition" in the Church also sometimes "means simply customs and ideas which have grown up imperceptibly and been accepted more or less uncritically."[9] This corresponds to the second meaning.

In either sense of the word, tradition is a major factor in Church life. It is precious but also ambiguous. It always needs to be tested critically to see "(1) whether it is in accordance with the principles embodied in divine revelation, and (2) whether it can be justified by right reason."[10] The Church can come to a judgment that some particular feature of "the tradition" needs to be modified in accordance with these criteria.

---

8    *The Oxford Dictionary of the Christian Church*, 2nd ed. edited by F.L. Cross & E.A.Livingstone (Oxford University Press, 1974, 1983), p. 1388.
9        Ibid.
10       Ibid.

Tradition (in its Christian meaning), is best understood as the process by which the Church keeps its sense of identity by remembering and staying in continuity with its beginnings—in faithfulness to the New Testament writings—while changing and developing in its understanding and living out of the faith.

The Church itself could be regarded as a "living tradition" that is able to persist and continue only by creatively re-thinking and re-appropriating its heritage, in response to the ever-changing cultures in which it exists.

Where is the Church's tradition to be found? One must look to the history of the Church, which, of course, is still continuing. This is a process that began two thousand years ago, so that "locating" and assessing it necessarily involves a lot of historical study and work with documents of the past.

When we look closely at this history, we have to recognize that the Church has grown in its understanding and living of the faith, as it has taken on new forms of thought and cultural expression.

The first big transition came early, when the new Christian movement left its Jewish roots and began to be expressed in the cultural forms of the Greco-Roman world. This resulted, eventually, in the writings of the "Church fathers" of the early centuries (the "patristic" period) and in the doctrinal formulations of the Nicene Creed. We still look to that period as an important source of insight into the mystery of Christ.

Later, as the Roman Empire in the West collapsed under the impact of the barbarian invasions, the Christian faith there had gradually to express itself in the mentality and institutional forms of the Germanic tribes. After centuries of turmoil, a new synthesis eventually emerged in the thought and practices of the medieval Church.

This European form of Christianity has continued up until the present day, though drastically challenged and modified in various ways by the great intellectual and cultural movements of the past five centuries—Renaissance, Reformation, Enlightenment, and modern science. Christian believers have tried to understand and express their faith in relation to these new cultural and intellectual situations, and this task continues to occupy our best thinkers.

In all these developments, it is the process of "traditioning" that has enabled the Church to persist and continue. This has involved and still involves much more than compiling collections of teachings from past ages of the Church. The "living tradition" of Christian faith continues in the creative re-thinking of its basic beliefs and doctrines and in the creation of new forms of Church life.

How is tradition related to Sacred Scripture? Some have considered tradition to be a second and separate source of revelation alongside Scripture, but this is not the Anglican view of the matter. Rather, tradition is the Church's process of continually re-appropriating the meaning of the normative witness given in Sacred Scripture.

A helpful formulation of this point of view is found in the 1998 "Virginia Report" of the Inter-Anglican Theological and Doctrinal Commission:

> "Tradition refers to the ongoing Spirit-guided life of the Church which receives, and in receiving interprets afresh God's abiding message... Tradition is not to be understood as an accumulation of formulae and texts, but as the living mind, the nerve centre of the Church. Anglican appeal to tradition is the appeal to this mind of the Church carried by the worship, teaching and the Spirit-filled life of the Church." [11]

But what is to be done when sincere Christian believers disagree about what "the mind of the Church" is on some disputed question? This has happened, of course, more than once in the history of the Church, and it has often taken many years for the final resolution of an issue.

In order to recognize a valid development of the living tradition, the Church must always practice spiritual discernment. Christian believers seek to recognize the authentic leading of the Holy Spirit by staying together in prayer, Scripture study, and mutual charity, as they explore an issue. This requires patience and genuine openness to one another's insights and convictions.

The current controversy about sexuality is a case in point. The Church is presently faced with a cultural situation altogether different than anything envisaged in the cultures which produced the biblical

---

11    Quoted in *Some Issues in Human Sexuality* from the English House of Bishops (Church House Publishing, 2003), p. 51.

writings or in the cultures through which the Church has moved thus far. And so we are engaged in a very difficult spiritual discernment of how the living tradition about sexual morality should develop further. As we pursue this, we need to put our trust in the Holy Spirit who leads the Church into all truth.

Faithfully,

The Theologian

# Section 4: The Sacramental
# Life of the Church

The sacraments of the Church are treated here from an Anglican point of view, but the author's insight into this material developed over many years of teaching sacramental theology in the Roman communion.

# Baptism

Dear Theologian,

Why does our Church baptize babies? I can understand how meaningful Baptism is for an adult person or even a child. But what sense does it make to administer this sacrament to an infant who cannot know what it means? What effect do we think this has on a baby?

Wondering

Dear Wondering,

If we are to understand the meaning of Infant Baptism, we must first examine the rich and profound meaning of Adult Baptism, for this is the primary and normative form of the sacrament.

Let's begin with some basic principles of sacramental theology. According to the Catechism of the Book of Common Prayer, "The sacraments are outward and visible signs of inward and spiritual grace, given by Christ as sure and certain means by which we receive that grace." [12]

The use of an "outward and visible sign" to express something spiritual, personal and intangible is actually very common in human life. Because we are physical beings, we need to "embody" our thoughts, feelings and decisions. So, people smile, frown, shake hands, carry flags, wear rings.

In some cases, the sign does not merely refer to something personal and spiritual, but really does convey the unseen reality and make it able to be sensed, felt, touched and celebrated. The exchange of wedding rings by a bride and groom, for example, is a concrete, visible sign of their life-long commitment to each other.

From this perspective, we can better understand why the Church celebrates sacraments. They are symbolic rituals that embody and make tangible the spiritual reality of our profound relationship with God through Jesus the Christ in the power of their Spirit.

---

12      BCP, p. 857.

The initiative is from God, who calls human persons into the relationship. This possibility is offered as a generous, free, undeserved gift. Hence, we call it "grace." The human response to this gracious offer is called "faith."

The beginning of Christian faith-living comes by being initiated into the "KOINONIA" (communion) of the crucified and risen Jesus, the fellowship of new humanity that has been created by His life, death, and resurrection and the gift of the Holy Spirit.

In the case of an adult, this happens through a process of "catechesis" and preparation for Baptism, the sacrament of initiation. It involves a lot of learning —not merely of doctrines, but also of "habits of the heart," ways of behaving, choosing and loving. One gradually acquires the vision and values and purpose of the community that is the Church of Jesus.

When a person is judged to be ready, he or she receives the sacrament of Adult Baptism—a solemn, public celebration of that person's entry into the fellowship of Jesus. This symbolic ritual expresses, at one and the same time, both the reality of God's saving grace offered in Christ and the human person's free choice to respond in faith.

It is the natural symbolism of water that conveys the rich meaning of this event. Water can be used for washing or cleansing. So it is easy to see how being immersed in water could show outwardly the mystery of the forgiveness of sins and the washing away of the old life of evil and unbelief. *"Wash me thoroughly from my iniquity, and cleanse me from my sin."*(Ps 51:2)

But water can also symbolize death and destruction. To be submerged in water over your head is to be in danger of drowning. And uncontrolled, rushing water can carry away everything and drown anyone in its path. So, going down into the water can show outwardly the mystery of dying to one's old self and one's old way of life, as one is identified with the death of Christ. And coming up again out of the water can show outwardly the mystery of rising up to a new life in the power of the Spirit, as one is identified with the resurrection of Christ. (Cf. Rom 6:3-4.)

In the light of this symbolism, Baptism appears as a momentous event of surrender to God's grace and abandonment to God's power, letting go of one's old way of life, and making a profound personal commitment to a new way of life.

That is why adults who wish to take this step are first asked whether they renounce all evil, accept Jesus as their savior, put all their trust in his grace and love, and promise to follow and obey him as their Lord. Furthermore, they are asked whether they believe in God the Father, God the Son, and God the Holy Spirit. And they are invited to make certain promises, which we call "the Baptismal Covenant." [13]

But if all this is true of an adult being baptized, what are we to say of baptizing infants?

It is quite clear that an infant is not yet capable of making an act of faith or of committing self to a way of life. Nor does he or she yet have any personal sins to repent of or any "old way of life" to turn away from. None of this applies.

What is symbolized in Infant Baptism, above all, is the gracious initiative of God choosing and calling this person to belong to Christ and to become a member of his Church—long before he or she is capable of making any response to God.

What is also symbolized by baptizing the baby is his or her incorporation (as infant) into the Church. But this makes sense only if the adults involved (parents, godparents, Church community) are truly committed to raise this child in the Christian faith. And that is why the parents and godparents are asked the same questions that are posed to an adult person seeking Baptism. For it is really their faith into which this child is to be initiated.

The practice of Infant Baptism is legitimate, however, only if the baptizing faith community takes very seriously its responsibility to foster the spiritual development of the ones who have been baptized. The process of "catechesis," which for an adult precedes the ritual of Baptism, will have to take place after Baptism for those baptized as infants. This is why Christian education and formation are of such crucial importance for our children and young people.

---

13      Cf. BCP, pp. 304-305.

The practice of Infant Baptism without adequate Christian formation produces congregations of baptized people who have never undergone catechesis or initiation. This is a significant aspect of the present malaise of many Church communities.

Does baptizing an infant wrongly "pre-empt" his or her freedom to choose? Not really. When a person baptized as an infant reaches a point of sufficient maturity, he or she will need to make a choice either to affirm or repudiate the Baptism once received passively. Affirming one's Baptism is a serious moral decision because it involves a commitment to live by the Baptismal Covenant. Without that kind of personal commitment, one has not yet entered into the fullness of Christian faith-living—whether baptized as an infant, a child, or an adult.

In Christ,
The Theologian

# Confirmation

Dear Theologian,

Can you help me understand what our sacrament of Confirmation is really all about? When I was a Roman Catholic, I was taught that Confirmation confers the Holy Spirit upon a person. But now, in the Anglican communion, I'm told that it is the rite by which a person, originally baptized as an infant, publicly renews and re-affirms the Baptismal Covenant in a personally responsible way. Which explanation is (more) correct?

Somewhat Confused

Dear Confused,

Let me approach this question by putting it into a larger theological context. There are much deeper mysteries involved in this discussion than the history or theory of ritual.

Most basic of all is the Mystery of God, as known in Jesus of Nazareth (together with all that led up to him and all that has followed from him). In our cultural world, this Mystery must never be trivialized by taking it for granted while we argue about ritual and Church arrangements.

Rather, the question of God is the burning issue for all human beings today who seek meaning and purpose for their existence. How, many ask, is it still possible to believe in God, or to speak of God plausibly?

The question about God can never be answered theoretically in a satisfying way. Only people who bear witness to the divine Goodness by their values and behavior can make belief in God plausible to others.

The Church of Jesus is called to do this, to speak of God by its very existence, and to allow the reality of Jesus to continue to reverberate in history. As he was the supreme witness to the divine Goodness, even and especially in his helplessness and suffering, so also those who bear his name are to continue the witness.

Church, therefore, must be seen as implicated in the ultimate Mystery of God and the manifestation of that Mystery in Jesus the Christ. The Church can and must be understood as "the Body" (in Paul's sense), the corporate mystery of human beings who are being gathered, transformed, and re-created by the Holy Spirit, to be—as a community— the visible sign of Christ's presence to the world.

If Church is understood in this dimension, and not merely in its institutional and organizational features, then one can appreciate why initiation into it could be of enormous human significance. And only then can the discussion of Confirmation be appreciated properly as the effort to understand how each member is to enter more deeply and authentically into the fellowship of the Crucified and Risen One.

Christian Initiation is the process by which an individual is brought into the corporate mystery of the Church. It is important to distinguish at least two aspects of this: (1) the actual process of instruction and formation by which a person gradually takes on the vision, values, and behavior of the Christian "Way" (2) the sacramental ritual of Initiation whereby the entry of a person into full communion with the Body is symbolized, enacted, and celebrated.

In the early Church, Initiation was celebrated sacramentally in one unified rite (water Baptism, followed immediately by laying on of hands, with or without anointing, and admission to the Table of the Eucharist). The symbolic force of the laying on of hands (sometimes with anointing) immediately after Baptism was to impart the "seal of the Spirit."

A distinct rite, believed to impart the Holy Spirit at some time later than Baptism, came into being gradually, as a kind of accidental development in the Western Church. This happened because of the insistence that only the Bishop could perform that part of the original unified baptismal rite. This led to postponement of the concluding ceremony of Baptism for ever-increasing periods of time—ultimately, for years.

Consequently, what had originally been an intrinsic moment in the entire baptismal liturgy now came to be felt as a separate and distinct rite. Because the ritual of laying on of hands, often with anointing, had originally symbolized the gift of the Holy Spirit within the unified initiation liturgy, theologians tended to attribute to the separated ritual the efficacy of conferring the Holy Spirit.

Hence the medieval "sacrament" of Confirmation was believed to impart the Holy Spirit in a new way, beyond the efficacy of Baptism, conferring upon a person at the threshold of adulthood special gifts and "strength for the battle" (*robur ad pugnam*) of Christian life. This continues to be the Roman Catholic understanding of the sacrament of Confirmation.

The distinctive Anglican conception and practice of Confirmation came into being in the 16th century, influenced by the continental Reformers.

A close examination of the rite of Confirmation in the Prayer Books of 1549, 1552 and 1662 shows the attempt to combine a new function of Confirmation (the reaffirmation of baptismal vows at a mature age by a person baptized as an infant) with the old liturgical form of the medieval sacrament of Confirmation (which signified the imparting of the Holy Spirit).

Thus, two quite different and unrelated functions of "Confirmation" were combined uneasily in one ritual. This is the ambivalent heritage with which Anglican theologians, liturgists, and pastors have had to wrestle in modern times.

From our present vantage point, the effort of medieval theologians to attribute to Confirmation a new gift of the Spirit (beyond the bestowal of the Spirit in Baptism) seems to be simply a misunderstanding.

On the other hand, the ritual of laying on of hands with anointing really does have baptismal meaning (as it did originally, when it was not yet removed from its full liturgical context). That is, it is an extension of one very important meaning of Baptism: the gift of the Holy Spirit.

Not all the meanings of Baptism are symbolized by the Confirmation ritual, of course. But the meaning of being given the Holy Spirit is clearly expressed, and offers the possibility of saying Yes in freedom to this gift once given, of receiving it actively in a stance of faith which really affirms the entire commitment of a Christian.

Rightly understood, therefore, the apparent anomaly of Confirmation (as an accidentally detached symbolic fragment of the baptismal liturgy) can serve to confront a mature person with the reality of his/her Baptism.

This "extension" of Baptism into a time when the baptized is capable of an act of faith really allows him/her to relate with deliberate choice to a sacrament celebrated originally without his/her personal participation.

Faithfully,

The Theologian

# Holy Communion

Dear Theologian,

When I was growing up in the Episcopal Church, the Book of Common Prayer contained an order of service for "the Lord's Supper or Holy Communion," although some parishes preferred to call it "the Mass." At present, the Prayer Book calls it "the Holy Eucharist."

Is there some important spiritual or theological meaning in this variety of names? How are they related to one another?

Bewildered by All the Changes

Dear Bewildered,

What we do with bread and wine on Sunday morning is the heart and center of Christian existence. That it should be called by several different names is perhaps not so surprising, when one considers the long and varied history of Christianity. Each of the names highlights a somewhat different aspect of an infinitely rich mystery.

Although this central ritual of Christian faith has taken on many different cultural forms—some quite elaborate—its essential structure is actually simple. The celebrant takes bread and wine, says the great blessing prayer, breaks the bread, and distributes the bread and wine to all the participants.

We might characterize this simple sequence of actions as a symbolic meal, with the elements of food and drink reduced to a small, token amount for each person. But what does it mean?

Its meaning is to be found in its origins. When the first Christian believers began gathering in the name of the crucified and risen Jesus, they would share meals together in the Jewish way. At the beginning, they would say a blessing over the bread, then break and share it. At the end of the meal, they would bless a cup of wine and share it. In this familiar pattern of interaction, they were remembering Jesus and relating to him as present in the power of the Spirit.

In one of the earliest New Testament texts we have (Paul's First Letter to the Corinthians, written perhaps around 54 AD), we find a precious interpretation of what was then being called "the Lord's supper." Paul attributes the origin of this ritual to Jesus himself *"on the night when he was betrayed"* (1 Cor 11:23-26) in a passage which is strikingly paralleled in the later writings that we call the Gospels (Lk 22:14-20, Mt 26:26-28, Mk 14:22-25).

According to this account, Jesus took the traditional Jewish table ritual and gave it a new, unexpected meaning. As they ate the one bread that he blessed and broke (and later, as they drank from the one cup of wine that he blessed), they were given a share in his self-giving sacrifice that was about to be made *("my body given for you ... my blood poured out for many")*. The basic meaning of this symbolic action, therefore, was about his disciples participating in the great mystery of his sacrificial death.

Those who participate in the Church's ongoing celebration of this mystery are opening themselves to being united with the crucified and risen Jesus. Eating the consecrated bread and drinking the consecrated wine in the attitude of reverent faith is an act of intimate communion with the Lord. It is rightly called Holy Communion.

But there is another reason for using the word "communion" for this ritual of sharing together in the great mystery of Christ. The New Testament word KOINONÍA, often translated as "communion" or "fellowship," means precisely "having something in common, sharing in something." It is by sharing together in the Christ mystery that many human beings, in all their diversity, are gathered into communion with one another.

This is celebrated and, indeed, enacted again and again, whenever believers gather for the symbolic meal of bread and wine, blessed and shared in Christ's name. The "communion" of the Church is continually created anew when this happens. The ritual thus has a "Church-forming" function.

What about "the Mass"? This name, used by Roman Catholics as well as many Anglo-Catholics, is derived from the Latin word *missa* in the ancient words of dismissal or "sending forth" at the end of the celebration. *("Ite, missa est!")* In traditional Roman Catholic doctrine, the word occurs typically in the phrase, "the holy sacrifice of the Mass."

In this Catholic understanding, the mystery of Christ's death is interpreted as the perfect sacrifice (of himself) by which he reconciles sinful humanity with God. Offered once and for all on Calvary, this same eternal sacrifice is made present sacramentally in every celebration of the Mass—so that the participants can share in its benefits and unite themselves to Christ in their own self-offering. Rightly understood, this Catholic doctrine is quite compatible with the Anglican understanding. [14]

What about the name "Holy Eucharist," which is used widely today by Anglicans and others? "Eucharist" is from the Greek word that means "giving thanks," a word still used in modern Greek as the everyday expression for "thank you!" When addressed to God, the word expresses the glad recognition that everything is grace (sheer, unmerited gift from God).

When the Christian community gathers in the name and power of Jesus, its fundamental stance is this joyous, deeply grateful praise of God. It is expressed richly in the blessing prayer chanted or recited by the celebrant of the Eucharist, which is called "The Great Thanksgiving." We praise and thank God for creating the entire universe, including ourselves, and above all for redeeming us through the life, death, and resurrection of Jesus.

Our gratitude and praise pass over naturally into the humble offering of ourselves—our life, our energy, our talents—to be spent for God's purposes. And we do all this consciously in union with Christ our brother and Lord. It is summed up in the final words of the great prayer: "By him, and with him, and in him, in the unity of the Holy Spirit, all honor and glory is yours, Almighty Father, now and for ever. AMEN." [15]

All this meaning is included in the sacramental event which then follows. Uniting ourselves with Christ as we eat the one bread and drink from the one cup, we are also united with one another, to be Christ's Body in this world. What we are doing is, at the same time, "Holy Communion," "Sacrifice" and "Holy Eucharist."

Faithfully,

The Theologian

---

14     Cf. Rite I: *"Accept this our sacrifice of praise and thanksgiving, whereby we offer and present unto thee, O Lord, our selves, our souls and bodies."* BCP, p. 342.

15     BCP, p. 369.

# Real Presence

Dear Theologian,

What does the Episcopal Church teach about the "real presence" of Christ in the sacrament of Holy Communion? When I was growing up in the Roman Catholic Church, I was taught that the bread and wine were changed into the actual body and blood of Christ. Now, as an Episcopalian, I am told that we reject this idea of "transubstantiation" (so-called). But how do we understand the Lord's presence in the sacrament?

Doubtful Communicant

Dear Communicant,

In thinking about the Holy Eucharist, we are attempting to think about "Mystery" in the strict theological sense—that is, a reality that is forever beyond our full comprehension, even though we can get some partial understanding. Therefore our thinking and speaking must be done with great reverence and humility.

The Church's faith in the "real presence" of Christ in the sacrament of Holy Communion is grounded in Scripture and attested by many patristic writers of the early centuries. In a famous passage, St. Paul writes (sometime in the decade of the 50's AD):

> *"The cup of blessing that we bless, is it not a sharing in the blood of Christ? The bread that we break, is it not a sharing in the body of Christ? Because there is one bread, we who are many are one body, for we all partake of the one bread."* (1 Cor 10:16-17)

A little further on in the same letter he writes:

> *"Whoever, therefore, eats the bread or drinks the cup of the Lord in an unworthy manner will be answerable for the body and blood of the Lord."* (1 Cor 11:27)

The vivid sense of the "objective" reality of Christ himself in the eating and drinking of the consecrated elements has persisted down through all the centuries. In the medieval period, however, an extreme literal understanding of this presence became fixed in the popular mind, so that the consecrated bread itself was sometimes imagined to be the actual body of Christ in a physical sense.

Beginning in the eleventh century, the doctrine of "transubstantiation" was formulated as a way of affirming the real presence. Using philosophical concepts that were current at the time, this doctrine affirmed that the "substance" of the bread and wine was, by the power of God, converted or changed into the "substance" of Christ Himself, even though the "accidents" (appearance, taste, etc.) of bread and wine remained.

This theology was accompanied by a popular piety which was focused on the consecrated bread as object of devotion. People longed to gaze upon the elevated Host when it was lifted up by the priest after the words of consecration in the Mass. The Host was also put on display for adoration at certain times, and was even carried in procession. On the other hand, the people rarely if ever received Holy Communion; only the priest consumed the consecrated elements.

It is generally recognized today that this medieval Eucharistic piety was a distortion of the sacrament. Part of the program of the Reformers in the sixteenth century was to restore the integrity of the Eucharist by encouraging the people to receive Communion and to understand the liturgy as a sacred meal (the Lord's Supper).

Why did the Church of England reject the concept of "transubstantiation"? Article XXVIII of the Articles of Religion (as reaffirmed by the Episcopal Church in 1801) says: "Transubstantiation (or the change of the substance of Bread and Wine) in the Supper of the Lord, cannot be proved by Holy Writ; but is repugnant to the plain words of Scripture, *overthroweth the nature of a Sacrament*, and hath given occasion to many superstitions." [16]

The words singled out above for emphasis get at the heart of the matter for Anglicans. It is in "the nature of a sacrament" that the natural or physical reality remains itself, while at the same time making present the spiritual reality. The bread is still bread, after the prayer of consecration, but now it is also a sacrament in the sense that it makes present a spiritual reality.

"The outward and visible sign in the Eucharist is bread and wine, given and received according to Christ's command. The inward and spiritual grace in the Holy

16    BCP, p. 873, emphasis added.

Communion is the Body and Blood of Christ given to his people, and received by faith." [17]

This statement of the Eucharistic faith of the Episcopal Church clearly affirms the spiritual reality of Christ's self-gift to his people when the sacrament is received in the attitude of faith. But it also makes clear that the bread and wine function sacramentally as "the outward and visible sign."

The Anglican perspective on the Eucharist can be appreciated better by looking at the theology of Richard Hooker (1554-1600).

> "Like Cranmer, Hooker's doctrine can be described as a doctrine of the real partaking of the body and blood of Christ in the Eucharist, rather than a doctrine of the real presence of Christ in the Eucharist. This doctrine of the Eucharist, which became characteristic of Anglican theology, is often referred to as 'receptionism.' Hooker does not deny the real presence, but he relates it primarily to the faithful communicant rather than to the elements of bread and wine... On the question of the relation of the presence to the elements of bread and wine he adopts a position of deliberate agnosticism: '...what these elements are in themselves it skilleth not, it is enough that to me which take them they are the body and blood of Christ.'" [18]

This understanding of the Eucharist shifts the emphasis away from the elements in themselves (as a possible object of devotion) and views them rather in their sacramental function as communicating the presence of Christ to the one who receives them in the attitude of faith. This is in accord with Cranmer's effort "to reorient Eucharistic doctrine around the act of Communion, rather than around a change in the nature of the elements." [19]

What Anglican and Roman Catholic Christians have in common, despite differences in terminology, is the centrality of the Holy Eucharist in their life of faith. Christ's presence in this sacrament remains a great Mystery—to be entered into, but not to be explained.

Faithfully,

The Theologian

---

17    In the Catechism of the Book of Common Prayer, BCP, p. 859.
18    W. R. Crockett, in *The Study of Anglicanism*, revised ed., pp. 309-310.
19    Ibid., p. 309.

# Sacrifice

Dear Theologian,

There's a part in Rite I of the Holy Eucharist that I would like to understand better: "Here we offer and present unto thee, O Lord, our selves, our souls and bodies, to be a reasonable, holy, and living sacrifice unto thee."[20] What does it mean to offer our souls and bodies to God? How are we supposed to do that? And what does it mean to say that we want "to be a reasonable, holy, and living sacrifice" to God?

A Worshiper

Dear Worshiper,

The phrasing from Rite I of the Holy Eucharist Prayer that you quote above is based on a passage in St. Paul's Letter to the Romans:

> *"I appeal to you therefore, brothers and sisters, by the mercies of God, to present your bodies as a living sacrifice, holy and acceptable to God, which is your spiritual [or: reasonable] worship."* (Rom 12:1)

For Paul, the word "body" (SŌMA) does not refer to one part only of the human totality, but rather to the complete person seen from one point of view: the point of view in which the human being exists within the world of space, time and matter, within the multiple pressures and temptations that this places upon him or her.

It is this bodily self that is to be "presented" to God as "a sacrifice." The word "sacrifice," of course, would in the ancient world carry the connotation of animal sacrifice. But here Paul apparently means something quite different, since he calls this a "living sacrifice." It is the way that the human bodily person lives in this world that constitutes his or her offering to God.

He calls this kind of self-offering *"spiritual worship"* (LOGIKÉN LATREÍAN). An equally good translation of the Greek phrase

20     BCP, p. 335.

would be: *"reasonable worship."* It is the kind of worship that is in accordance with reason. The Jerusalem Bible translation offers a helpful paraphrase in this sense: a worship *"that is worthy of thinking beings."*

What kind of worship is that? It might help to continue our reflection on this by considering a passage in Eucharistic Prayer B of Rite II: "We offer our sacrifice of praise and thanksgiving to you, O Lord of all." [21]

What is this "sacrifice of praise and thanksgiving" that we say we are offering to God? If it is to be more than mere words, it must take the form of a sincere and whole-hearted dedication of our entire lives to the love and service of God. This is expressed clearly in Morning Prayer II:

> "Give us such an awareness of your mercies, that with truly thankful hearts we may show forth your praise, not only with our lips, but in our lives, by giving up our selves to your service, and by walking before you in holiness and righteousness all our days." [22]

So we are called to worship God not merely by ritual acts (like the celebration of the Eucharist), but more profoundly by living according to the will of God.

True "surrender" to God turns out to involve a more and more complete self-giving to others, as we imitate and share in the self-giving Love that God is. This can take many forms, but always feels like a kind of "dying" to our own will.

It is this spiritual meaning of "sacrifice" that Christian faith sees in the life and death of Jesus. He *"became obedient to the point of death, even death on a cross."* (Phil 2:8) He gave himself away, without remainder. He let go of everything in order to be faithful to the incomprehensible will of the Father.

Christian faith rejoices in the utter goodness and rightness of Jesus' surrender to the Father, and sees in this great act of self-giving the overcoming of all human estrangement from God.

To belong to Christ, through Baptism, is to share more and more fully in his eternal "sacrifice" of self-giving love. This is why we not only remember gratefully the sacrifice of Jesus but also beg to

21     BCP, p. 369.
22     BCP, p. 101.

be included in it, as we yield our lives more fully to the blessed will of the Father. "Unite us to your Son in his sacrifice, that we may be acceptable through him, being sanctified by the Holy Spirit." [23]

Sincerely,

The Theologian

---

23      BCP, p. 369.

# The Table of the Eucharist

Dear Theologian,

In the front of every one of our Churches there is an altar. As an old-timer, I remember when it used to be against the east wall of the Church. The priest would stand facing the altar, with his back to us. But now I hear people calling it a "table," and the priest stands behind it, facing us. Why the change? And what is the difference between calling it an altar and calling it a table?

Person in the Pews

Dear Pew-Person,

The form of Eucharist with which many of us grew up was the inheritance of the medieval period of Western Christianity. It must be recognized frankly that this form of the Eucharist was far removed in outward appearance and in spirit from the "primitive Eucharist" of the first believers.

In the very earliest days of the faith, the symbolism of a shared meal was uppermost in the outward form of the Eucharist. This style of celebration was believed to derive from the Lord himself, who had instituted it at his Last Supper with his closest disciples.

At that meal (which may have been a Passover meal), Jesus had taken a familiar Jewish table ritual and given it a new depth of meaning with reference to himself and his imminent death for the sake of his friends. Sharing in this symbolic meal, then, was the ever-repeated occasion when the early believers entered into the meaning of his life and death, experienced his risen presence in their midst, and committed themselves to live by his way.

In the medieval period, when very few of the laity even received Communion, the meal symbolism was preserved only in an atrophied form insofar as the priest-celebrant consumed the consecrated bread and wine. But what was uppermost in the medieval form of the Eucharist was the theme of "sacrifice."

The priest was believed to offer up to God, in an "unbloody" way, the very same infinitely precious sacrifice which once was offered up in a bloody way on Calvary. Or, putting the matter more carefully, the same Christ who offered himself once and for all to the Father (for the salvation of all mankind) was believed now to be making his eternal sacrifice present, in the symbolism of the Mass and through the ministry of the ordained priest, for the benefit of those assembled.

In this understanding of the ritual of the Mass, the table where the bread and wine were placed was thought of as an altar, on which the sacrifice was offered.

Until the liturgical renewal of the twentieth century, all Catholic Churches (Anglican as well as Roman) had an altar against the back wall of the sanctuary, often very ornate and imposing. In a sense, the altar symbolized the Mystery of God, toward which the whole congregation was oriented, and which the priest approached reverently in the name of the people.

The fact that the priest had his back turned to the people showed that he was there not primarily to dialogue with them or even to address them, but rather to lead them into the holy presence of God and to offer on their behalf the Sacrifice of the Mass. The people's part was to look on with faith and devotion, and to join themselves in spirit with what was being done on their behalf by the ordained priest.

The renewed theology and practice of the Eucharist in both the Anglican and the Roman Churches has returned to the biblical meal symbolism of early Christianity. In so doing, the significance of the altar/table has changed considerably.

Churches built since the renewal ordinarily reflect the new understanding and practice in their physical arrangement of space. Older Church buildings are adapted as well as possible to the new form of Eucharist, either by moving the original altar out into the middle of the sanctuary, or (if this is not possible) by setting up a table as close to the body of the congregation as possible (leaving the original altar in place as a kind of backdrop).

The essential symbolism of the Eucharist, in its renewed form, is that of a shared Meal in which all participate. The focal point of the assembled congregation is now a table, on which are placed ordinary, basic food and drink (bread and wine) in plain view of all, with the obvious purpose of being provided for everyone eventually to eat and drink together.

Before sharing this symbolic Meal, a great prayer of praise and thanks is intoned at the table by the person who is "presiding," in order to express the deep religious meaning of the Meal, and in order to give voice to the faith and love of all those who are gathered around the table. At its conclusion, the entire assembly sings or says "Amen!" to express their agreement and conviction.

Notice the different function of the priest-celebrant in this form of the Eucharist. He/she is there to focus the faith of the assembled people, to give voice to it, and to draw all of them together around the one table, in readiness to "take and eat." The priest-celebrant is not doing something on their behalf, namely, offering a sacrifice which they are not empowered to offer. Rather, he/she is leading a great communal action, which all those present are doing together.

One final point: Granted that the outward form of the Eucharist is now much more clearly that of a symbolic Meal, what has happened to the theme of "Sacrifice"?

The theme of Sacrifice is still expressed in some of the prayers, even though the outward action itself no longer thematizes this meaning so explicitly. In fact, the deepest meaning of Jesus himself and of his death is "redemptive sacrifice"—a handing-over and abandonment of himself to the Father, in which all men and women are somehow included, so that they are reconciled in principle to the God from whom they have been willfully estranged.

This loving abandonment to the will of the Father, this gift of self to God, is really the "essence" of the crucified and risen Jesus upon whom the community feeds, with whom the community is joined in the sacred Meal.

"Sacrifice," therefore, is a major theme in the meaning of participating in the Meal. By sharing in the Lord's Supper, we all freely share in his Sacrifice and are caught up into his own eternal act of loving surrender to the Father on behalf of the world. But the outward, symbolic form of our identification with Jesus' Sacrifice is the form which he himself chose to give us: the simple, ordinary behavior of breaking bread together at his Table.

Faithfully,
The Theologian

# Marriage as Sacrament

Dear Theologian,

Is Christian marriage a sacrament? Our Catechism calls it a "sacramental rite."[24] But what does this mean? How is Christian marriage an "outward and visible sign of inward and spiritual grace"?

A Married Believer

Dear Believer,

The marriage of a man and a woman is an occasion for the Church to celebrate the mystery of its own covenant relationship to Christ. This understanding is expressed in our liturgy for the celebration and blessing of a marriage: "The bond and covenant of marriage … signifies to us the mystery of the union between Christ and his Church." [25]

To appreciate how and why this is so, we should begin by asking just what is meant by "marriage."

In the West, the essence of marriage has come to be regarded as the consent of two people to be husband and wife—the establishment of a contract. While the exchange of vows may certainly be regarded as the moment in which the marriage is publicly sealed, there is much more to a marriage than the consent.

A new history is to follow from that act of consent. In this perspective, marriage can and must be regarded as the whole life of married love—a process of growing union between two human beings. This involves fidelity and the gradual growth of a true community of life.

Why does the Church regard marriage—understood in this fuller sense—as a "sacrament"? What is the hidden spiritual reality which is signified and symbolized when two baptized persons commit themselves to a life-time of faithful love?

---

24    BCP, p. 860.
25    BCP, p. 423.

We can only appreciate the profound spiritual meaning of Christian marriage when we situate it in its full context. This is why the ritual for the celebration and blessing of a marriage ordinarily takes place within a celebration of the Holy Eucharist.

The human reality of the joining of a man and a woman—placed in this context—turns out to have a revelatory power. It shows a depth of meaning, in relation to the mystery of God. This couple's love for each other (here and now ritualized) is a sign of the far greater mystery of Christ's covenant love for his Church.

In this way, the couple themselves can sense and rejoice in the depth meaning of their act of freedom, and can see their union as a sign of the union of Christ with the Church. And for the faith community which celebrates with them, this man and woman—joined—are a sacrament of the ultimate mystery of God which encloses and supports the entire community.

The couple themselves celebrate (and thus "receive") the Sacrament of Marriage. They do this in the larger context of meaning provided by the covenant community. The priest is present to be the official witness of their marriage. And there is an assembly of believers gathered also as witnesses. One might say that the local Church thus "con-celebrates" the Sacrament of Marriage with this couple.

What is the "effect" of the Sacrament of Marriage for the couple? What is "the inward and spiritual grace" that is given to them when they participate in this "outward and visible sign"?

Their love for each other is now located within the divinely established covenant community. Their marriage is now supported by Christ's faithful love for his Church. They take on a new shared reality and status within the faith community, and draw strength and courage from the faith and good example of the other members of that community.

Is this kind of effect negligible? By no means. Consider how empty and "thin" a wedding can be when there is no community to celebrate the deep human and divine meaning of what the couple are doing. Consider how difficult it is to remain faithful in a permissive society without the support and good example of other married people in a community.

Thus, the grace of God works in and through the human realities of the Church, of its rituals and of its shared life. God works, of course, in countless ways in the lives of the couple. Always, though, the renewing and "saving" of their marriage is a matter of rediscovering and living the themes celebrated in the ritual. In that sense, it is a matter of the "grace of the sacrament" being renewed again and again.

Faithfully,

The Theologian

# Forgiveness

Dear Theologian,

I grew up in the Catholic Church, where we were told to "go to confession" to a priest fairly often, to have our sins forgiven. Do we have anything similar in the Episcopal Church? How are we to find forgiveness for our sins?

A Penitent

Dear Penitent,

Your first question can be answered simply. Yes, the Episcopal Church does have something very similar to the Roman Catholic Sacrament of Penance, now usually referred to as Reconciliation. You can find it in the Book of Common Prayer at page 447, under the heading "The Reconciliation of a Penitent."

Like many other practices in the Anglican form of Christianity, this rite is available to all who request it from a priest, but is not required of anyone. The decision to request it is left up to the discernment of the individual believer. A familiar saying applies here: "All may, none must, some should."

Your second question, though, demands a fuller response. How, indeed, are we sinful human beings to find forgiveness for our sins? The question becomes intensely personal for each one of us at certain times, when we become aware of how little we have responded to the infinite Love that is at the heart of things.

The way into finding forgiveness begins when we take the time to enter humbly into the presence of the One who loves us absolutely. There are no preliminaries necessary. It is not as if we had first to get our house in order, through moral conversion and change, before God would be willing to love us and come to us.

We need, however, first to learn to be quiet enough to hear the voice of God affirming and accepting us as we are. The discipline of silence is required. But we must also read Sacred Scripture and believe in the Word of God, especially as it reveals the infinite mercy that attends us.

Only after we have allowed God to love us for a while, should we then direct our attention to that self which is so dear to us and at the same time so wounded and unloving. We can dare to look at ourselves as we are, if we are illuminated by the light of God's love directed to us seemingly unlovable ones.

The self-knowledge that we then gain can, however, lead us to want to hide ourselves from God, because we are actually so unworthy to be in relationship to that furnace of love. How can we dare to turn towards the Light? What gives us the hope that we will be healed and renewed in that Light, rather than destroyed by it?

Here it is important to remember that we stand in a great fellowship of forgiveness. The gracious, forgiving Love that God is, has brought into being a community of forgiven people which extends through all times and places and even includes the dead. And each of us is a member of that fellowship.

It is in and through the liturgical and sacramental life of the Church community that we receive the revelation of God given to us in the Sacred Scriptures of Israel and of the Church. The place in which we hear the Word of divine forgiveness, and are able to believe in it and allow ourselves to be forgiven, is the fellowship of forgiven sinners who belong to God through the reconciling death of Christ.

This happens again and again, whenever we gather with fellow believers to celebrate the Holy Eucharist. The Word that is read and proclaimed prepares us to be forgiven and reconciled with Christ in the Sacrament. It is true to say that the primary Sacrament of forgiveness, after the once-and-for-all event of Baptism, is the Eucharist.

Why, then, does the Church provide a separate and distinct rite for the Reconciliation of a Penitent? And when is it appropriate?

Persons who have been guilty of serious moral failure have a special need for an individual, personal, extended rite of reconciliation— in order to experience their own sorrow and to experience the overwhelming goodness and mercy which surrounds them and allows a new beginning (in spite of everything).

Why is this valuable? Because it takes the whole process of forgiveness out of the seemingly merely private and inward sphere, and places it in the public, social context of the community of faith to which the person belongs. There is an objectivity about celebrating the Sacrament of forgiveness which greatly strengthens a person's faith and allows him or her to feel in a bodily, interpersonal way the reality of being forgiven.

What does the Sacrament involve?

It is an act of faith, an expression of worship, entered into with a fellow believer who, by virtue of ordination, represents the entire fellowship of forgiven sinners. In a setting of simple faith and honest prayer, the two listen to the Word of God and put their absolute trust in the divine forgiveness.

Then the penitent confesses in specific terms the nature and shape of his or her sins. Why this? Because, as the famous 5th Step of Alcoholics Anonymous has demonstrated for millions, to admit to another human being the exact nature of one's failures allows one to admit it fully both to one's self and to God. And without that full and honest admission, no one can ever change or be healed.

The priest may then respond with some words of counsel and encouragement, and ordinarily also imposes some small but significant action to be carried out later as an expression of one's sincere repentance and desire for amendment of life.

Finally, the priest solemnly utters the words of forgiveness and release, of pardon and peace. He absolves the penitent in the name of the Church and therefore in the name of Christ from whom the Church lives. This is a word of authority, to be accepted gladly by the one who has entrusted himself or herself so completely to the mercy of God:

"Our Lord Jesus Christ, who has left power to his Church to absolve all sinners who truly repent and believe in him, of his great mercy forgive you all your offenses; and by his authority committed to me, I absolve you from all your sins: In the Name of the Father, and of the Son, and of the Holy Spirit. Amen."

The words of forgiveness are accompanied by a gesture—the priest extends a hand over the penitent, and may lay a hand on the person's head or shoulder.

The final words of the priest sum up the significance of what has occurred:

"Now there is rejoicing in heaven; for you were lost, and are found; you were dead, and are now alive in Christ Jesus our Lord. Go in peace. The Lord has put away all your sins." [26]

Faithfully,

The Theologian

---

26      BCP, p. 451.

# Anointing

Dear Theologian,

When my uncle was in the hospital with a serious illness, a priest came to visit him and anointed his forehead with oil. I know that this is one of the Church's sacraments, but I'm not sure that I understand its meaning. Why is it done, and what effect does it have?

Unsure

Dear Unsure,

To answer this question, we have to look briefly at the history of anointing in the Church. The classic text for this practice is in the Letter of James:

> *"Are any among you sick? They should call for the elders of the Church and have them pray over them, anointing them with oil in the name of the Lord. The prayer of faith will save the sick, and the Lord will raise them up; and anyone who has committed sins will be forgiven."* (Jas 5:14-15)

The symbolism of anointing with oil is easy to appreciate, since this is clearly an act of soothing and comforting. There is, however, hardly any evidence that the anointing of the sick was practiced as a liturgical ceremony performed by priests during the first eight centuries of Christianity. There is evidence that oil was blessed by the bishop and was used by the faithful as a kind of remedy for illness (not merely by anointing the body, but even by tasting and consuming the oil). The significant thing was the blessing of the oil by the bishop, which made the oil itself the bearer of sacred power.

Beginning around the ninth century, there was a formalizing of the ritual of anointing, and it was reserved for the priest to perform. Around the same time, this anointing began (apparently for the first time) to be closely associated with deathbed penance and the immediate preparation for death.

This development was complete and taken for granted by the time the theology of the sacraments was worked out by the scholastic theologians in the twelfth and thirteenth centuries. Hence, the meaning attributed to this anointing was almost exclusively the consecration of the person for death, the "last anointing" (*extrema unctio*).

This understanding of anointing made the appearance of a priest at the sickbed an omen of impending death. Hence, people postponed the anointing as long as possible, since having it done was equivalent to giving up all hope. Thus, what historically was originally a sign of comfort and hope had become a sign of death, inspiring terror.

It must be recognized that the concept of "last anointing" was a secondary development, to be understood in terms of the historical circumstances of the Dark Ages. The theology of the scholastics was simply an interpretation of a practice that they took to be immemorial. But now—with the aid of better historical knowledge—we can see that this theology is not well founded in either Scripture or the first eight centuries of the Tradition.

Therefore, a contemporary theology of the sacrament of anointing puts the emphasis once again on the healing and strengthening of a person who is seriously ill (whether or not at the point of death). But how are we to understand this ritual, and what effect is it thought to have?

When one is seriously ill there is weakness, pain, a sense of mortality. Even if one is not in immediate danger of death, the fragility and finitude of one's human condition is experienced very strongly. The ultimate reality of death is somehow present in one's awareness. At the same time, one is estranged and alienated from the normal world of work, play, interpersonal contacts and interactions. One lies isolated. One is dependent on others, yet somewhat cut off from them.

In such a situation the believer very much needs to interpret all this in the context of explicit Christian faith. But it is precisely when one is ill that prayer and faith sometimes become difficult, if not impossible. One feels the need for a vision of faith, but is often unable to rise to that level of awareness.

In view of this general situation of the sick person, the Church has a "ministry" to those of its members who are sick. This ministry involves "visiting the sick," in order to take care of that person's needs in whatever way is most appropriate. Medical attention is normally provided by health-care professionals. What is not ordinarily provided by doctors and nurses is meaning. What does all this suffering and helplessness mean? How can one understand his or her situation in relation to God?

The Church ministers to this need for meaning when its members come to visit the sick person. In many cases, it is the priest or deacon who comes, representing the entire faith community. He or she does not provide glib, ready-made answers, but makes present the good news of Jesus through conversation and reading of Scripture, and by praying with this person.

All this ministry receives a ritualized, sacramental expression in the sacrament of the anointing of the sick. This ritual will be most meaningful, in fact, only if there is such a context of pastoral care of the sick person. Without such a context, the simple action of anointing will probably not have the same depth or resonance of meaning.

The sacrament of anointing, therefore, communicates meaning by relating this person's suffering to the Paschal Mystery of Christ (his death and resurrection). Moreover, the representative of the faith community who comes to visit helps the sick member to overcome the experience of isolation and estrangement that goes with being sick. The visitor embodies for him or her the faithful love of the Father, as revealed in the Son.

Now, instead of experiencing estrangement, one can experience connectedness, acceptance, love, and oneness with the community. Through this, he or she can be reassured of being enfolded in God's love and cared for. He or she may be brought to the point of surrender in faith, of abandonment to God's love.

In this attitude of faith, one is open to the healing power of God, and physical healing sometimes follows. The same attitude of radical openness to God can, however, also lead to a peaceful sharing in the mystery of Jesus' death, as one hands over his or her life completely to the God who has raised Jesus from the dead.

All this is appropriate to any situation of serious illness, even if there is no question of the immediate danger of death. Of course, it is also appropriate if a person is near death. In fact, the mystery of death announces itself in any serious illness, and the logic of faith is always the same.

Faithfully,
The Theologian

# Section 5: Pastoral Theology (the Christian Life)

In this section, the questions have to do with various aspects of living the Christian faith. They are not arranged in any particular order, but the reader might want to look at the table of contents to identify topics of interest.

# Bible as Word of God

Dear Theologian,

In our Sunday worship, at the end of each reading from the Bible, the reader says solemnly "The Word of the Lord." What does this mean? Do we believe that everything in the Bible is truly a direct word from God?

Dubious Hearer of the Word

Dear Hearer,

In thinking about the Bible as "the Word of God," we need to keep in mind how the biblical texts were written and how they were recognized as sacred. What we now regard as one book is actually a collection of books (the word "Bible" is derived from the plural Greek noun *BIBLIA*, meaning "books"). Where did these writings come from?

Let's begin with what we call "the Old Testament."

The writings gathered together to form the Hebrew Bible are the product of a people living through a troubled, unpredictable history. These texts were composed over a period of about a thousand years, and many individuals had a hand in the transmission of oral and written materials, in the combination and editing of these materials, and in the final "redaction" of each book. The Hebrew Bible can be regarded as the Book of a People, since its writings were produced out of the common experience of this people in history.

There is an over-arching narrative, as well as laws, poetry, prayers, wisdom literature, etc. What emerges with striking originality, out of all these writings, is a unique, transcendent Person who creates, saves, shapes and re-shapes a people to know his Name and to belong to him in a covenant relationship. "You shall be my people, and I shall be your God."

At the same time, there is a very rich depiction of all the human responses, along the way, to this divine initiative. It is the story of an entire people living in relationship to the God who chooses and creates them to be a people. There are many fascinating individual stories, as well as the great lines of the people's history.

It is a story of human weakness, infidelity, and malice—as well as faith, trust, and love. It is a love-story, in which the divine Lover continually woos and courts a fickle, unsteady Beloved (the People of Israel). In the vicissitudes of their history, they come to an ever deeper and purer understanding of the God of their lives. The faith of Israel is refined in the fire of suffering and loss.

The first believers in Jesus of Nazareth (all of them Jews) regarded these Hebrew Scriptures as sacred, and sought in them prophecies that could be seen to be fulfilled in the life, death, and resurrection of Jesus. In effect, this was their way of recognizing and believing that Jesus' life and terrible death were the continuation and, indeed, fulfillment of God's action in the history of their people.

How was the "New Testament" written and eventually established as authoritative for the Church?

The earliest Christian writings which later became regarded as "Scripture" were the letters of Paul the Apostle to various Churches in the Mediterranean world. The gospels were written later than Paul's letters—putting into final written form the older oral and written traditions about Jesus that had been circulating for many years. All the writings which are now regarded collectively as "the New Testament" had been written by the end of the first century or the early years of the second century.

For a long time, however, there was no official list of Christian writings that were to be regarded as Sacred Scripture. And even when such lists began to be compiled, there was some variation as to what should be included. The present "canon" (definitive, authoritative list) of the New Testament writings was not settled by the general authority of a council until late in the fourth century.

It was only through this long history that "the Bible" came into being. It is true to say that "the people of Israel" wrote the Hebrew Bible and that the early Christian communities ("the Church") wrote the New Testament. Moreover, in each case it was the community of faith itself which eventually established a definitive canon of the writings it would regard as sacred and authoritative for its life of faith.

If this is how our Bible came to be, doesn't it seem to be all too human, both in the writing of its texts and in how those texts were judged to be sacred? What can be meant by saying that the Bible is "the Word of God"?

Many Christians regard the Bible as the literal word of God. In this view, the text of the Bible is divinely given in its every detail, and completely without any error (at least in its original version). The entirety of the text and all parts of it are regarded as the very word of God, as God intends it to be heard.

"Inspiration" is thought of as God's influence upon the minds of the writers, infallibly causing them to write only what God wanted written. Hence, the Bible may truly be considered "God's Word written." This view is held by many evangelical Christians, including some in the Anglican communion.

This strict literalist view, however, has become untenable for many other Christians (Roman Catholics, some main-line Protestants, and some Anglicans), because the application of the critical-historical method to the writings of the Bible has shown just how human they are.

As Reginald Fuller, an Anglican scripture scholar, notes:

"...the Bible is ... a very human product, the work of many human authors over a period of a thousand years or more, and all of them conditioned by the cultural assumptions of their age. Biblical criticism has further shown that the Bible is a highly pluralistic work, containing the personal views of many different writers, views that are shaped by the particular situations in which they were written." [27]

In such a view, can the Bible be said to *be* the Word of God? It seems that one would rather have to say something like this: the Sacred Scriptures, in all their variety and with all their human qualities, *contain* the Word of God. The truth and holiness of God shine through the texts, despite their human limitations.

We are left, therefore, with very different understandings of "the Word of God" in the Bible. This is the underlying factor in many of

27    Reginald Fuller, in *The Study of Anglicanism*, ed. Stephen Sykes & John Booty, 1988, pp. 79-80.

the arguments among Christians today about various points of faith and morals.

In the literalist view, one can legitimately cite particular verses or passages (even out of context) wherever they occur in the Bible, as having the absolute authority of direct divine utterance. This allows one to make decisive judgments on particular points of doctrine and ethics.

In the critical-historical view, one must look to the overarching themes and principles that run through the varied writings, in order to make judgments about disputed points of doctrine and ethics. Particular texts are interpreted in the context of the larger whole, and full account is taken of the cultural limitations of some passages.

Can Christians of such differing views of the Bible find common ground on which to stand, as they dialogue about controversial issues? This is a question of great importance for the future of Christianity.

Faithfully,

The Theologian

# Why History

Dear Theologian,

I often find the Bible readings at the Sunday Eucharist hard to understand, especially those from the Old Testament. There seems to be an awful lot of specialized historical knowledge needed in order to make sense out of these ancient texts. My question is this: Why is there so much complicated history involved in our religion? Can't we just worship God in the here and now, without having to learn so much about the past?

Don't Know Much About History

Dear Don't Know Much,

Your question touches upon an area of crucial importance for the life of the Church. We read aloud from the Sacred Scriptures of the Hebrew Bible and the Christian New Testament at every Sunday celebration. But what effect upon the spiritual life of our people does this have?

The fact is that many (or even most) of the people in our congregations really do not know very much about the origin, context, and nature of the readings that are proclaimed in the liturgy. Since most of the time no introduction to these texts is given before they are read aloud, the readings can "go by" almost meaninglessly. On the other hand, if there is a proper introduction before a reading that does give the information needed to understand the text, it can sometimes seem like a history lesson.

Then why do we keep reading and trying to understand these texts from the past? To answer this question, we have to consider the fundamental, paradoxical nature of Christian faith. This way of being religious is oriented permanently to certain unique events of the past, and particularly to the life, death, and resurrection of one particular human being, Jesus of Nazareth. Historical reality is intrinsic to Christian faith.

Jesus is not a myth, nor is he a merely legendary figure. He really lived in the region now called "Palestine" at a period about which a great deal is known. The oral traditions about his life found a permanent written form not more than about forty years after his death (Mark). Scholars today are agreed that Mark is the earliest of the four "gospels." Other accounts were written some twenty to thirty years later (Luke, Matthew, John). It is from these gospels that we read every Sunday, because we need always to orient ourselves toward Jesus' unique human reality.

But Jesus did not appear out of a vacuum, nor did he come from some other world. He was born into a people with a long history, and we cannot begin to understand him without viewing him in the context of his people Israel. This is why we always take as our first reading each Sunday a selection from the sacred writings of the Hebrew Bible. We reverence these writings as the inspired record of God's action in history, creating and choosing a people to bear witness to God throughout the centuries. We attend not only to the original meaning of these texts for Israel, but also to the ways in which they point forward toward Christ.

In addition to the four gospels, the New Testament also contains a number of letters written by St. Paul and others to the early Christian communities around the eastern Mediterranean and at Rome. We take as our second reading each Sunday a selection from this material. Paul's letters, written earlier than the gospels, are a precious witness to the essential themes of Christian faith and contain valuable teaching on how to live the Christian life.

As you point out, many if not all of these biblical readings are very hard to understand without some specialized historical knowledge. This is why serious study of the Bible is needed, as a major part of Christian formation. But it is sadly lacking in the lives of many of our people.

We do, of course, often use the term "Bible Study" to refer to any kind of gathering to read and talk about biblical passages, with a view to discovering their relevance for the people gathered. But this kind of sharing, valuable as it may be, is really not true "study" of the Bible unless it is guided by some serious intellectual effort of the participants.

As Peter Gomes observes,

"Bible study actually involves the study of the Bible. That involves a certain amount of work, a certain exchange of informed intelligence, a certain amount of discipline. Bible study is certainly not just the response of the uninformed reader to the uninterpreted text, but Bible study in most of the Churches has become just that—the blind leading the blind..." [28]

Attention to the past is inescapable for Christian believers, especially in their efforts to understand and live by the Sacred Scriptures. But it would be a mistake to think that Christian faith is oriented merely to the past.

In attending to the past, Christians are looking at the earlier stages of a great process of creation and redemption that still continues in the present. It began unimaginably long ago, took shape in the history of Israel, and culminated in the life, death and resurrection of Jesus. Now it goes forward into the future. Each new generation is touched and enlivened by the Holy Spirit, in order to participate in the further unfolding of God's purposes (the coming of the Kingdom of God).

When we gather for worship we read from the ancient Scriptures in order to learn about the great "salvation history" that is continuing in our own lives of faith. We study the Scriptures that bear witness to what God has done, so that we can be conscious participants in what God is doing now. Remembering what has been enables us to be attentive to the grace of God in our own "here and now."

Faithfully,
The Theologian

---

28     Peter J. Gomes, *The Good Book: Reading the Bible with Mind and Heart* (New York: William Morrow & Company, 1996), pp. 11-12.)

# Salvation

Dear Theologian,

Someone asked me recently, "Are you saved?" I wasn't sure what to say in response. Thinking about it later, I realized that I didn't have a clear idea of what it means to be "saved." Yet I know that we Christians talk a lot about "salvation" and "being saved." I need some explanation of what these words really mean. Can you help?

Untaught Believer

Dear Untaught,

"Salvation" is a word that corresponds to the deepest longing of the human heart. What it signifies is in some sense the ultimate concern of all religion.

We know that all is not well with us. Injustice, oppression, and manifold forms of suffering characterize our social world, and each of us struggles against our own tendency toward evil. At the same time, we yearn for wholeness, for complete well-being of body, mind, and spirit—both for ourselves and for all human beings. We yearn for "salvation." Where is it to be found?

The answer given in the Hebrew Bible is clear and unequivocal. It is God alone (the LORD) who saves—from all forms of evil. *"Turn to me and be saved, all the ends of the earth! For I am God, and there is no other."* (Isa 45:22) *"I, I am the LORD, and besides me there is no savior."* (Isa 43:11)

The root of the Hebrew words translated by "save" and "salvation" has the basic meaning "to be broad," "to become spacious," and from this underlying meaning comes the idea of rescuing or delivering from some confining, threatening situation. For example, *"The LORD brought me out into a broad place; he delivered me, because he delighted in me."* (Ps 18:19)

Most references to "salvation" in the Hebrew Bible have to do with being rescued from physical danger in this present life, although we Christians often "spiritualize" the meaning of "salvation" when we encounter the word in the Psalms or the Prophets. Sometimes, of course, the word does refer to the final consummation of God's reign on "the day of the Lord," which will include the establishment of righteousness.

In the New Testament, most uses of the Greek word SOZO ("to save") and its derivatives, especially the noun SOTERIA ("salvation"), have a spiritual meaning, referring to the ultimate redemption of human beings in Jesus the Christ. But there are also places in the gospels where the word refers to a physical healing. For example, when Jesus says to people just healed, *"Your faith has saved you,"* the Greek word could just as well or more correctly be translated *"has made you well."* (Mk 5:34, 10:52) .

In the New Testament writings as a whole, it is clear that "salvation" for all human beings is achieved through the death and resurrection of Jesus. The meaning of this "salvation" is the establishment of the right relationship to God. Closely related concepts are "atonement," "reconciliation," "redemption," and "the forgiveness of sins."

From this perspective, the Reign of God has already been established, in principle, by what has happened in the life, death, and resurrection of Jesus. In that sense, "salvation" has been objectively achieved for all human beings. They have, in principle, been "saved" from their sinful estrangement from God.

But there is also a "not yet" dimension to this salvation. We are oriented in hope toward the complete establishment of God's Reign at the end of time. The consummation of salvation exceeds human ability to grasp it (1 Cor 2:9-10); in the present, the gift of the Spirit is a foretaste of what is promised and hoped for (Rom 8:23, 2 Cor 1:22, 5:5; Eph 1:14).

For us who are still in the midst of our "journey," therefore, there is also a sense in which we are still in the process of being saved as we move toward the ultimate fulfillment of God's salvation. As St. Paul writes,

*"I want to know Christ and the power of his resurrection and the sharing of his sufferings by becoming like him in his*

*death, if somehow I may attain the resurrection from the dead. Not that I have already obtained this or have already reached the goal; but I press on to make it my own, because Christ Jesus has made me his own."* (Phil 3:10-12)

From God's side, we might say, our salvation is assured, because of the saving death and resurrection of Jesus. From our side, though, there is still need of much learning, suffering, and transformation as we keep repenting of our sins and turning again and again to say Yes to God's holy will.

We encounter here, once again, the paradox of Grace and human freedom. The two sides of the paradox are well expressed by St. Paul:

*"Therefore, my beloved ... work out your own salvation with fear and trembling; for it is God who is at work in you, enabling you both to will and to work for his good pleasure."* (Phil 2:12-13)

"Are you saved?" You can reply with the assurance of faith that you have indeed been saved by God through the death and resurrection of Jesus, and through your Baptism and profession of faith in him. You can add that you are also still in the process of being saved, as you strive through your faithful choices to appropriate the "objective" salvation achieved in Christ.

Faithfully,

The Theologian

# Putting On Christ

Dear Theologian,

I have a question about a verse of Scripture that was read in Church recently: *"Put on the Lord Jesus Christ, and make no provision for the flesh, to gratify its desires."* (Rom 13:14) What does it mean to "put on" the Lord Jesus Christ? And how can one attempt to do that?

Mystified Disciple

Dear Disciple,

St. Paul understands the Christian life in terms of the most intimate possible identification with the crucified and risen Jesus. The metaphor of "putting on Christ," as one might put on a garment, seems to express the deliberate choice to identify with him. But this is, at the same time, a "putting off" of one's sinful behaviors. The verse you quote is preceded by these words:

> *"Let us then lay aside the works of darkness and put on the armor of light; let us live honorably as in the day, not in reveling and drunkenness, not in debauchery and licentiousness, not in quarreling and jealousy."* (Rom 13:12b-13)

Putting on Christ is closely linked, in St. Paul's writings, with the mystery of Baptism. *"As many of you as were baptized into Christ have clothed yourselves with Christ."* (Gal 3:27) But this means being identified with Christ's death and resurrection.

> *"Do you not know that all of us who have been baptized into Christ Jesus were baptized into his death? Therefore we have been buried with him by baptism into death, so that, just as Christ was raised from the dead by the glory of the Father, so we too might walk in newness of life. For if we have been united with him in a death like his, we will certainly be united with him in a resurrection like his."* (Rom 6:3-5)

Baptism is the beginning of a life that is "clothed with Christ," but this identification with him is to increase in depth and intensity throughout the believer's life. On the one hand, of course, all this is totally the work of God. On the other hand, it involves the ever-renewed free choice of the believer to be thus transformed. Hence St. Paul often urges and exhorts his people to make that choice (as in the verse you are asking about).

Perhaps we can get some insight into the "how" of putting on Christ if we look at another text of St. Paul. In Philippians 2, he is urging his people to be of one mind and heart, and to relate to one another with humility, rather than selfish ambition or conceit. Then he writes:

> *"Let the same mind be in you that was in Christ Jesus, who, though he was in the form of God, did not regard equality with God as something to be exploited, but emptied himself, taking the form of a slave, being born in human likeness. And being found in human form, he humbled himself and became obedient to the point of death—even death on a cross."* (Phil 2:5-8)

We are urged to have "the mind of Christ." And in another context, Paul even says that we do already have it: *"... who has known the mind of the Lord so as to instruct him? But we have the mind of Christ."* (1 Corinthians 2:9-11,16)

What is "the mind of Christ"? Only those who love him can begin to know, as they share ever more fully in his risen life. But we might get some understanding if we ponder the mystery of his being Son. At his baptism, the voice of God says: *"You are my Son, the Beloved; with you I am well pleased."* (Mk 1:11)

We ourselves share in this dimension of the Lord's being. When we accept Jesus as the Christ and are baptized "into" him, each of us becomes, in a profound way, "son" or "daughter" and we experience the divine acceptance. It is as if the Father says also to each of us: "You are my beloved son/daughter, in whom I am well pleased."

As this awareness grows in us, we can begin to live increasingly "from" the Father, as Jesus himself did. We can become more and more aware of our utter, absolute dependence upon God for all things. Attitudes that accompany this awareness are wonder, praise, gratitude, confident dependence and trust. To live this way is to be set free from undue anxiety.

As we try consciously to live the new Christ-life, we come also to recognize that we desire to do God's will, to let God's Kingdom come and be realized in us and in our world. The attitude is well expressed in what Jesus says to his disciples when they want him to eat the food they have brought: *"I have food to eat that you do not know about.... My food is to do the will of him who sent me and to complete his work."* (Jn 4:32,34)

As the Holy Spirit works in our lives, we also understand better the teachings of Christ and find that we desire increasingly to live by them. The way of being human that is revealed in Jesus, in his parables and in his actions, becomes the pattern for our own efforts to live with integrity and compassion.

"Putting on Christ" in this way, we too, like God's holy ones in all generations, may come to reveal in our lives something of God's peace and joy, God's justice and God's mercy. We can learn to be simply present and available to our fellow human beings—to love and serve them in practical ways. We can learn to be peace-makers who do not return evil for evil but rather overcome evil with good and repay hatred with love. When we suffer, we can learn to go through our ordeal in union with the suffering Christ, not giving way to bitterness or despair.

When we are urged to "put on" Christ, we are being invited into all this, and much more. It is utterly beyond our ability, yet we are summoned to cooperate with God's grace in our own transformation.

Faithfully,

The Theologian

# Lord

Dear Theologian,

What does the word "Lord" mean? It comes up in the Psalms and many other places in the Bible. We use it in our liturgy and in our personal prayers. But I am often uncertain of its application. When we say, "O Lord," are we addressing God (the Father)? Are we addressing Christ? Are we addressing the Holy Spirit? Does its meaning shift, from one context to another?

Needing Clarity

Dear Needing,

Let's begin with Scripture. In the third chapter of the Book of Exodus, when Moses encounters God in the burning bush, he asks what God's name is. The mysterious answer is usually translated "I AM WHO I AM" or perhaps "I WILL BE WHO I WILL BE." The voice of God goes on to say, *"Thus you shall say to the Israelites, 'I AM has sent me to you."* (Ex 3:13-15)

The sacred name of God, therefore, seems to be connected with the Hebrew verb HAYAH, "to be." It is written as YHWH, but is never pronounced aloud by devout Jews, out of reverence for the divine name. Instead, wherever it occurs in the text, a different word is substituted in reading aloud—ADONAI—which is translated as "Lord."

This is why most modern English translations of the Bible use the word LORD (in small or large caps) wherever the sacred name YHWH occurs in the text of the Hebrew scriptures. Therefore, when we encounter in the Bible this special usage of the word "Lord," whether in direct address or in narration, we need to remember that it represents the ineffable sacred name of God as revealed to the nation of Israel.

Why was it the word "Lord" that was substituted for

YHWH? In a male-dominated world of strong leaders and rulers, it perhaps was natural to use that word to refer to God.

On the other hand, "Lord" (apart from its special use to indicate the sacred name) is only one of many image-words used for God in the Old Testament. Moreover, it is important to realize that "Lord," like all the other "names" of God, is used only symbolically and metaphorically. God is not to be thought of literally as a bigger-than-life Commander or Master.

Yet something true and important is expressed through this particular metaphor. God is absolute source and last end of all that is.

> *"I am the LORD, and there is no other. I form light and create darkness, I make weal and create woe."* (Isaiah 45:6-7)
> *" Listen to me, O Jacob, and Israel, whom I called: I am He; I am the first, and I am the last."* (Isa 48:12-13)

When the Hebrew scriptures were translated into Greek, two to three centuries before the birth of Jesus, the translators chose the Greek word KYRIOS ("Lord") to substitute for the sacred name.

In the New Testament, it is this same Greek word that is used to refer to Jesus and to address him. If we assess this usage against the background of the Hebrew scriptures, it seems to apply to Jesus the word previously used (religiously) only to refer to the God of Israel (whose sacred name must never be pronounced aloud). This is a daring and startling use of traditional language, since it seems to equate Jesus, in some way, with YHWH.

A key text for pondering this is Philippians 2:6-11.

> *"Being found in human form, he humbled himself and became obedient to the point of death—even death on a cross. Therefore God also highly exalted him and gave him the name that is above every name, so that at the name of Jesus every knee should bend, in heaven and on earth and under the earth, and every tongue should confess that Jesus Christ is <u>Lord</u>, to the glory of God the Father."* [Emphasis added]

There is another way of looking at the significance of calling Jesus "Lord" if we situate this in the context of the Roman-ruled Hellenistic world in which the New Testament was written. In that world, the Greek word was used to refer to the Roman Emperor, and there was a cult of the Emperor in which honor was paid to him as divine. In such a context, to call the crucified and risen Jesus KYRIOS was a bold claim. It could be and was seen as a rejection of the Emperor cult, and an affirmation that it was really the risen Jesus who was now Lord of all things.

With all this in mind, let's turn to the questions you raise. Underlying these questions is the paradox that is at the heart of Christian faith. How can Jesus and God be so connected that the very same word ("Lord") used for God is also used for Jesus?

It has been difficult from the very beginning to sort this out. The Church struggled in the early centuries to reach a balanced and orthodox confession of faith. Despite the careful phrasing of the Nicene Creed, however, there can still be extreme misunderstandings of what authentic Christian faith is directed towards.

On the one hand, a kind of "Jesus-olatry" is possible, in which Jesus is simply regarded as God. On the other hand, it is also possible to reduce the significance of Jesus to something other than or less than God.

So, to whom are we praying when we say "Lord?" If we are not always sure of what we mean when we say, in prayer, "Lord," it is because Christian prayer is inescapably trinitarian in its orientation. This shows up most clearly in our liturgy. The Church prays to the Father "through" Jesus Christ the Son, in the power of the Holy Spirit.

At various moments in our journey of faith, we may well address either the Father or the Son or the Holy Spirit as "Lord" of our life. And in each instance, the word is appropriate.

To address the Father as "Lord" is to acknowledge the absolute sovereignty of the Creator and Giver of all things. This is expressed powerfully in the opening words of Gerard Manley Hopkins' poem "The Wreck of the Deutschland": "Thou mastering me God! giver of breath and bread; world's strand, sway of the sea; Lord of living and dead."

When, in Baptism, we acknowledge Jesus Christ as "Lord," we are submitting ourselves to his absolute authority (the very authority of God) and committing ourselves to live by his teaching and his values, to follow and obey him.

When, in the Nicene Creed, we confess our faith in "the Holy Spirit, the Lord, the giver of life," we are acknowledging our utter dependence upon the life-giving and life-changing power of God active within us.

Finally, how is it when we talk *about* "the Lord?" What reply can we give to the question, "Just who or what are you talking about?" The response has to come from the deepest part of ourselves, and the effort to clarify our meaning may well lead us into the depths of mystery, the paradox of God becoming man and the ineffable reality of the Holy Trinity.

Faithfully,

The Theologian

# Fear of the Lord

Dear Theologian,

There are many verses in the Bible that tell us we are to fear the Lord. Some examples are Psalms 22:23, 25:12 and 33:8. How can I fear the Lord and at the same time love and trust Him? Isn't this contradictory?

Wanting to Trust

Dear Wanting,

Here is another text that may offer a hint on how to approach this question: *"The fear of the Lord is the beginning of wisdom."* (Prov 9:10 and Ps 111:10)

First of all, just what is meant here by "fear of the Lord"? This is the emotion that is felt when a human being has a genuine and profound experience of God. It is a kind of awe-struck reverence in the presence of the Holy. It was felt by Moses at the burning bush (Ex 3), by Isaiah in his temple vision (Isa 6), and by John on Patmos (Rev 1).

When confronted inescapably with the reality of the Holy, a human being typically reacts with humility and a kind of self-abasement. This is often linked with the awareness of personal sin and unworthiness. (Simon Peter to Jesus: *"Go away from me, Lord, for I am a sinful man."* Lk 5:8)

This kind of "holy fear" is not to be confused with the ordinary fear that is felt in the presence of a hostile person or some other imminent danger. It is not terror, but rather a reverential awe before the unimaginably great reality of the living God.

Why is this holy fear called the beginning of wisdom? Because it brings a person into the attitude of humility and reverent openness to God without which no further learning about God is possible. But it is only the beginning of wisdom, because there is so much more to learn about God, as one is attentive to God's gracious self-disclosure.

When we consider how God has been revealed to Israel and the Church, we discover a further, wonderful dimension of the Holy. God is revealed as utterly gracious, merciful, faithful and trustworthy.

Here is a classic expression of what Israel came to know about God:

> *"The LORD, the LORD, a God merciful and gracious,*
> *slow to anger, and abounding in steadfast love and faithfulness,*
> *keeping steadfast love for the thousandth generation, forgiving*
> *iniquity and transgression and sin..."* (Ex 34:6-7)

Much later, the human figure of Jesus revealed in a new and incomparable way the "gracious" quality of the God before whom we tremble in holy awe. From Jesus' teaching and actions we learn to trust God absolutely as our Father. We also learn that we need not fear God's condemnation when we come, repentant, with our sins and guilt.

The greatest revelation of the gracious, faithful nature of the Holy has come in the glorious resurrection of the crucified Jesus. In this, God has vindicated his suffering servant and confirmed the truth of all that Jesus had taught by word and action. Jesus' resurrection shows us that it is right to trust utterly in the Father, even in and through the pangs of death.

In the light of revelation, then, we learn not only that we can trust the One before whom we feel "holy fear." We also learn that these two attitudes (fear and trust) need to be held together in creative tension.

If I tried to trust God without any "holy fear," I might well be putting my trust in some finite object of my own imagining. Any "god" with whom I could be totally "comfortable," with no sense of reverence, would be an idol.

On the other hand, if I could not trust the Holy One whom I sense in moments of "holy fear," I would have to live in anxious avoidance of that awesome reality. In fact, all of us have probably done this more than once in our own pilgrimage of faith.

The corrective for both of these one-sided approaches to God is to be found in the authentic revelation given to Israel and the Church. We need to let ourselves be guided by this, through a continual immersion in the Sacred Scriptures of the Old and New Testaments, as interpreted in the fellowship of the Holy Spirit (the Church).

But you may still feel the difficulty of holding fear and trust together in your way with God. How is this possible? For Christians, it is possible because of their union with Jesus the Christ. He affirmed fully Israel's "fear of the Lord" when he rejected the temptations of the evil one (Mt 4:1-11). At the same time, both then and throughout his living and his dying, he was ruled by utter, unqualified trust in the One whom he called "Abba" (Father). We who are members of his Body are given by the Holy Spirit a share in his blessed way of being human.

Faithfully,

The Theologian

# Hope

Dear Theologian,

Scripture says, *"Faith, hope, and love abide, these three."* (1 Cor 13:13) But what is meant by Christian hope? And how is it related to faith?

Hoping

Dear Hoping,

Let's begin with the ordinary meaning of the word "hope" in the English language: As a verb, it means "to wish for something with expectation of its fulfillment; to look forward to something with confidence or expectation."

This stance seems to be basic to human nature. We are beings who live always in expectation of something more than what we presently have or are. If we stop hoping, we are close to giving up on life altogether.

What is meant by Christian hope? In the New Testament letters, the Greek word ELPÍS, translated as "hope," occurs in many places. For example, *"Always be ready to make your defense to anyone who demands from you an accounting for the <u>hope</u> that is in you; yet do it with gentleness and reverence."* (1 Pet 3:15-16) This passage suggests that hope is almost a defining characteristic of the Christian believer.

What reason do Christians have for living with hope? We can best get at this by considering what those who first heard Jesus were hoping for. They belonged to a people who for five centuries had been longing for a future restoration of the Kingdom of Israel under the rule of a just and powerful king. For many, this included the expectation of an "anointed one" (*messiah*) who would be sent by God not only to restore Israel, but to bring in the new and final age—the age of God's justice and peace. (Look, for example, at the vision of "the peaceable kingdom" in Isaiah 11.)

When Jesus appeared, he proclaimed that "the Kingdom of God" was at hand. This must have re-awakened, for many, the never-abandoned hope of the restoration of Israel. But, as things turned out, Jesus did not bring about a military or political change of fortune for Israel. Rejected by his own people, he was executed as a criminal by the Romans who controlled the land.

What became, then, of the hope which his disciples had entertained? Their state of mind is poignantly expressed by the two disciples on the road to Emmaus: *"Our chief priests and leaders handed him over to be condemned to death and crucified him. But we had hoped that he was the one to redeem Israel."* (Lk 24:20-21, emphasis added) This expectation of theirs had been destroyed with utter finality by his death.

What, then, is the origin of Christian hope? We cannot understand it (or feel it) without believing in the resurrection of the crucified Jesus. It was only the revelation of the risen one that changed the disciples' state from despair to incredulous joy. And it is only our own faith in him as risen Lord that grounds our hope. As Paul saw so clearly, if Jesus is not risen, we have no hope.

> *"If Christ has not been raised, your faith is futile and you are still in your sins. Then those also who have died in Christ have perished. If for this life only we have hoped in Christ, we are of all people most to be pitied."* (1 Cor 15:17-19)

When we say on Easter Day "Alleluia! Christ is risen! The Lord is risen indeed! Alleluia!" (BCP, p. 294) we are not merely affirming that something is true (that Christ is risen). More fundamentally, we are putting our trust in the transcendent power and utter faithfulness of the God who has raised Jesus from the dead.

Abraham, for St. Paul, was the model of that kind of unshakable trust in God, when he dared to hope that God's promise of descendants would be fulfilled. He took this stand *"in the presence of the God in whom he believed, who gives life to the dead and calls into existence the things that do not exist."* (Rom 4:17) This is the "kind of God" that Christians also dare to believe in.

If faith, then, is understood as trust—indeed, total trust in God—then it is quite clear that faith is "the ground" of hope. Looking to an unknown future with firm hope is possible only because of one's confidence in the God who has raised Jesus from the dead. *"I know the one in whom I have put my trust, and I am sure that he is able to guard until that day what I have entrusted to him."* (2 Tim 1:12)

Christian hope, though not contrary to reason, can never be grounded rationally in a way that would rule out faith. I cannot be sure intellectually that my hope is justified. But when I put my trust totally in the God of Jesus Christ, I can be whole-hearted in living my life with firm hope, even in the face of death.

But what are Christians hoping for? In the familiar words of the Nicene Creed, recited every Sunday, "We look for the resurrection of the dead, and the life of the world to come."[29] This is the ultimate "object" of Christian hope, but it is not the only thing that we hope for. It is precisely our firm faith in the unimaginable future of the risen life that enables us also to hope for many things in this present life.

This is why Christians who are deeply rooted in the Lord can engage themselves in the struggles of the world without despairing. A person of faith is one who insists on living with hope, reaching out always to a future which is incalculable and uncertain, but which is in God's hands.

Hope, in a way, is the essential thing about the Christian outlook on life, in contrast to the absence of hope in much of our popular culture. Hope for ultimate joy in the risen Christ enables Christian believers also to hope for good outcomes of the processes of history. Even in the midst of defeat and suffering, the Christian never stops hoping, because the Christian's firm ground is the God of the crucified and risen Jesus.

Faithfully,
The Theologian

---

29    BCP, p. 358.

# Trust

Dear Theologian,

In Morning Prayer I came upon these verses in Psalm 146:

*"Put not your trust in rulers, nor in any child of earth, for there is no help in them. When they breathe their last, they return to earth, and in that day their thoughts perish. Happy are they who have the God of Jacob for their help, whose hope is in the LORD their God."* (Ps 146:2-4)

Scripture here seems to say that we should not put our trust in other human beings. But how is it right or even possible for us not to trust one another? And why should trust in God rule out trusting other human beings?

Trusting Soul

Dear Trusting,

What does trust involve? Here is a dictionary definition of the English word: As a noun it means "assured reliance on the character, ability, strength, or truth of someone or something." As a verb it means "to place confidence in, to rely on." Perhaps we could sum up this range of meanings with the colloquial expression, "to count on."

What does "trust in God" mean, in the context of the Psalms? There the term is closely related to another word, "refuge," that also occurs often. "The happy are those who 'take refuge in' God... happiness derives from living in complete dependence upon God rather than upon the self."[30] To take refuge in God is frequently expressed as putting one's trust in God. "To be happy is to entrust one's whole self, existence, and future to God." [31]

The kind of trust that the Psalms are speaking about (trust in God) is absolute and unqualified. Moreover, Scripture is saying that there is nothing except God that you can ultimately and completely rely upon. To put that kind of absolute trust in any created being is always wrong.

30    *The New Interpreter's Bible, Vol. IV* (Nashville: Abingdon Press, 1996), p. 666.
31    Ibid.

Are we being told, then, not to put any trust in fellow human beings? Are we to trust only in God in a way that rules out trust in one another? Common sense at once recognizes this as a false conclusion from the Scripture text.

We need to make a distinction between two quite different ways of trusting. On the one hand, there is the ordinary, every-day sense in which we put our trust in other people, as well as in our own faculties and skills. This is right and proper, and we cannot live without trusting ourselves and one another.

We know, however, that others can sometimes "let us down" by not living up to what we counted on them to be or to do, and that we ourselves do not always function as well as we expected to. Furthermore, as the Psalm says, human beings are mortal. In fact, all created things that we might "count on," such as money, power, beauty, possessions, are all transient and—in the end—unreliable. So it can only be a relative and conditional trust that we place in such things.

On the other hand, absolute and unqualified trust can be properly placed only in God. The passage of Scripture that you quote is really warning us against taking any finite, created being as the object of such absolute trust.

We need this constant reminder because in our sinful condition we are always inclined to put our total confidence in something finite and created. When we do this, we are in effect setting up an "idol."

There is a penetrating analysis of the forms that present-day idolatry can take in H. Richard Niebuhr's book, *Radical Monotheism and Western Culture*.[32] One form of idolatry that he identifies there which is especially noticeable in our present political situation is "nationalism." But there are many others.

Scripture unmasks our idolatries and summons us to worship the true and only God. Jesus' reply to the Tempter sums up the faith of Israel, which is also the faith of the Church: *"It is written, 'Worship the Lord your God, and serve only him.'"* (Lk 4:8)

---

32     New York: Harper & Row, 1943, 1960.

Worship involves a radical orientation of the human person to God as the only source of all that is good and as the ultimate end of all striving. We might call this stance "surrender to God."

Jesus lived this out, in all that he taught and did, and finally in the way his life ended. The Passion was the supreme test of Jesus' surrender to the Father. It was the culmination of a life that belonged wholly to God.

We who have been baptized into Christ are summoned to enter into his absolute, unqualified trust in the Father, no longer relying upon ourselves or anything created. But this does not come easily, and we can only grow gradually in this attitude. We may be given moments of special grace, when we are confronted inescapably with the need to surrender to God. Most of us could probably think of one or more situations in our life where this has been true. For all of us, the ultimate time of surrender to God will come with our dying.

We are to entrust our whole self, existence, and future to God. But this becomes agonizingly difficult when we experience weakness, pain, and suffering. Jesus himself was taunted by his enemies when he was helpless on the cross. *"He trusts in God; let God deliver him now, if he wants to; for he said, 'I am God's Son.'"* (Mt 27:43) Yet Jesus continued to trust, even unto death. *"Father, into your hands I commend my spirit."* (Lk 23:46) And it was by this trusting surrender to the Father's will that he entered into the unimaginable glory of the Resurrection.

To trust in God—even to "rejoice in God"—no matter what we are suffering, is possible only through the grace of God. It is a paradoxical stance, not to be accounted for through human reasoning. If our minds falter at the immensity of this challenge, we may find encouragement in these words of Scripture: *"Trust in the LORD with all your heart, and do not rely on your own insight. In all your ways acknowledge him, and he will make straight your paths."* (Prov 3:5-6)

In Christ,

The Theologian

# Judging Others

Dear Theologian,

How are we supposed to observe the commandment not to judge one another? *("Judge not, and ye shall not be judged." –* Lk 6:37) Don't we have to make distinctions between good and evil? And don't we have to make judgments sometimes about the character and behavior of other people? Are we supposed to simply close our eyes to immoral and unjust actions?

Judgmental Christian

Dear Judgmental,

Let's begin by making a distinction between "judgment" and "condemnation." We often think of judgment as essentially negative and condemnatory. But the word itself does not necessarily carry that meaning.

To judge means "to form an opinion or estimation of, after careful consideration." Judgment means "the act or process of judging; the capacity to form an opinion by distinguishing and evaluating; the capacity to assess situations or circumstances and draw sound conclusions." [33]

"Judgment" then is a matter of assessing situations and objects and forming a well-founded opinion about them. (We sometimes praise a person as "having good judgment.") Making judgments is natural and essential for human life. If we could not judge, we could not know anything with certainty.

But what about moral judgments? What about an "assessment" of a fellow human being which leads to an opinion about the morality of his/her actions and character?

It is legitimate and sometimes necessary to assess a person's actions and character. Not to do so, in some situations, would be irresponsible and imprudent (for example, in hiring someone). If the assessment turns out to be negative in certain respects, this is important knowledge, and need not be denied or ignored.

33    *The American Heritage Dictionary of the English Language, 3rd edition.*

What would it mean, though, to "condemn" another person, in view of the assessment made? "Condemnation" goes far beyond forming a correct opinion about the morality of another person's actions. It draws a conclusion about this person's total worth and ultimate destiny, and consigns him or her to fitting punishment (either in this life or the next).

Christians are, indeed, cautioned not to judge one another in this sense of condemning, for this kind of judgment is beyond the competence of human beings. It is only God who can judge a human person fairly and truthfully. For only God knows everything that is relevant to that judgment. Christians believe that all human persons stand under the final judgment of God, who is perfectly just and, at the same time, wholly merciful. (Cf. Rom 14:10-13.)

The verse from Luke's gospel that you quote occurs in a context that stresses the incomprehensible love of God for all human beings. It is this mystery which seems to lie behind the command not to condemn one another. Jesus is commanding his disciples to imitate the mercy of God.

> *"Love your enemies, do good, and lend, expecting nothing in return. Your reward will be great, and you will be children of the Most High; for he is kind to the ungrateful and the wicked. Be merciful, just as your Father is merciful. Do not judge, and you will not be judged; do not condemn, and you will not be condemned. Forgive, and you will be forgiven; give, and it will be given to you."* (Lk 6:35-38a)

The absolute, unrestricted, merciful goodness of God toward both good and bad human beings is at the heart of the Good News. A parallel passage in Matthew makes the same point:

> *"Love your enemies, and pray for those who persecute you, so that you may be children of your Father in heaven; for he makes his sun rise on the evil and on the good, and sends rain on the righteous and on the unrighteous."* (Mt 5:44-45)

Imitating the mercy of God does not mean ignoring the difference between "righteous" and "unrighteous" behavior. We surely have the right and obligation to make discriminating judgments about good and evil, both in ourselves and in others. But we are to love even those who do evil, and leave the final judgment of their lives to God.

Faithfully,

The Theologian

# Why Repeated Prayers

Dear Theologian,

If we really do believe that God answers our prayer requests, then why do we constantly bring our requests to Him? Why keep doing this over and over, especially for the healing of a beloved one? Aren't we to rest assured He will take care of it?

Puzzled

Dear Puzzled,

Why do we keep asking God for what we need? A simple answer is that we are following tradition. This way of persistently pleading with God is rooted in both the Hebrew Bible and the New Testament.

For example, in Lk 11:5-13 (with its parallel in Mt 7:7-11) is found the familiar exhortation of Jesus: *"Ask, and it will be given you; search, and you will find; knock, and the door will be opened for you."* The point is illustrated by a story about someone late at night bothering his neighbor for a loan of some bread until the reluctant neighbor finally gets out of bed and gives it to him. In Lk 18:1-8 Jesus tells a similar story—about an unjust judge who finally grants justice to a widow because she keeps coming and asking. He told them this parable *"about their need to pray always and not to lose heart."* (Lk 18:1)

But your question, I think, is seeking a rationale for this practice, a way of understanding it which coheres with our belief that God is responsive and faithful toward those who pray.

Why should we keep asking for what we need? Does God need to be "reminded"? Is this an attempt to "change God's mind," to persuade God to give us something that He otherwise would not? Or, worse still, is it an effort to "manipulate" God into doing what we want? To all these, Christian faith answers instinctively No.

But why, then? Perhaps there is a clue in the verse quoted above. The text speaks of _their_ _need_ to pray always. (emphasis added) God, to be sure, does not need to be asked, in order to render God gracious to us or to those for whom we pray. But perhaps we need to ask, in order to keep establishing ourselves in the right relationship to God.

The reiterated plea arises from our need to keep commending to God the one for whom we are concerned, to keep "holding" that person before God. Intercessory prayer, therefore, is a deep and sincere exercise of our own faith in God.

To pray for others is to entrust them to the unimaginable greatness and goodness of the One whom Jesus addressed as "Father." One cannot do this without at the same time entrusting oneself totally. It is a radical surrender, in faith, to the incomprehensible mystery of God.

What effect does such prayer have? It certainly has an effect on those who are praying. As we center ourselves in the Love which God is, we partake a little in God's totally affirming love of all creatures. Transcending our natural preoccupation with self, we realize that God loves the people we are praying for just as much as God loves us. How can we not open our hearts to them in compassion and solidarity?

To pray only once for someone, however, might leave our own hearts relatively untouched. But ever-repeated prayer for someone is bound to affect us deeply, and even lead to changes in our behavior. The transformed heart that is fashioned in such intercessory prayer finds ways to act on behalf of the needy. God's love for those in need is channeled through our human consciousness and choices.

There is also the possibility that our repeated praying for someone does somehow affect that person in a real and positive way. This is beyond our understanding, but we cannot rule it out. Standing in solidarity and love with the other person, before God, is a vital expression of the mysterious connection among all of us—what our Church tradition calls "the communion of saints."

These reflections may or may not provide a satisfying answer to your question. As always in theology, we are involved in talking about what is too great for us to understand fully. But we can always come back to the clear teaching of Jesus, who encouraged us to keep asking, seeking and knocking, and not to lose heart.

Faithfully,

The Theologian

# Idolatry

Dear Theologian,

In the Ten Commandments, the people of Israel were forbidden to make "idols" (images) or to worship them. Does this commandment have any relevance for people living today in our Western culture?

Bible Interpreter

Dear Interpreter,

The people for whom those commandments were written lived in a mental world of many gods and goddesses. It took Israel a long time to come to the belief that there is only one God. In the earlier stages of their history, they were really "henotheists," meaning that, although they believed in the existence of many gods, they were committed to worshiping only one.

The first two commandments seem to take for granted the existence of "other gods," even though worshiping any of them is strictly forbidden.

> "I am the LORD your God, who brought you out of the land of Egypt, out of the house of slavery; you shall have no other gods before [or "besides"] me. You shall not make for yourself an idol, whether in the form of anything that is in heaven above, or that is on the earth beneath, or that is in the water under the earth. You shall not bow down to them or worship them; for I the LORD your God am a jealous God." (Ex 20:2-5)

Later, of course, Israel came to a purified faith that is expressed in the great prophets.

> "Thus says the LORD... There is no other god besides me, a righteous God and a Savior; there is no one besides me. Turn to me and be saved, all the ends of the earth! For I am God, and there is no other." (Isa 45:18,21-22)

The classic expression of Israel's faith in one God is the "Shema" text, recited daily by observant Jews:

> *"Hear, O Israel: The LORD is our God, the LORD alone. You shall love the LORD your God with all your heart, and with all your soul, and with all your might."* (Deut 6:4-5)

Authentic Christian faith also affirms the utter uniqueness of the one and only God. Is, then, the commandment not to worship "other gods" irrelevant for us?

Not really, because the worship of "substitutes for God" is a constant temptation of the human heart. We yearn for something that we can get our hands on, so to speak, and be sure of. And even if our "idol-worship" is not so crass and obvious as bowing down before a wooden image, it may well take the form of a total absorption in some limited object of devotion—whether that is another person, the nation-state, money, sex, or fame.

If we look to any finite reality for the total meaning of our existence, and if we give to any finite reality our total loyalty, we are—whether we think of it that way or not—really fashioning an "idol" for ourselves.

The word for this kind of fanatical devotion to a merely finite cause is "idolatry." Anything or anyone whom we absolutize as the object of our total loyalty becomes an "idol" (a substitute for God).

It is much easier to recognize idolatry when the object of loyalty is clearly something "secular" or worldly: a nation-state, a political party, a cause, a family, financial success, power over others, etc.

It is not so easy to recognize the more subtle idolatries that occur within Church life, because the objects of loyalty seem so closely associated with God. People may identify totally with a particular charismatic leader, a powerful preacher, hierarchical office-holders (popes, bishops), the teaching authority of the Church, a particular local congregation with its unique history, a particular tradition and style of worship, a particular edition of the Book of Common Prayer, or even the Bible itself.

All of these can be and often are invested with such absolute importance that they crowd out of people's consciousness the overriding claims of God. God is so identified with a tradition, an authority, a book, a particular leader that no other mediation of God can be recognized or honored.

How do we unmask idolatry, especially in the life of the Church?

When we look at the life of any congregation, we can say this: One sign of loyalty to God (beyond all idols) is "oneness of heart." Devotion to the true God opens people's hearts to one another in mutual humility, respect, and loving care. On the other hand, a clear sign that people are overly devoted to "idols" is a state of division, mistrust, hostility, and even contempt between individuals and factions within the community.

Life in the Spirit of God involves an endless process of purification from idols. We need not be surprised that we are idol-worshipers. This is our natural condition as sinful people. The good news is that God is continually at work in our lives to set us free from our idolatries, to purify our lesser loyalties until our full loyalty is given to God alone.

This is a life-long process. We are not immediately set free from all our worship of idols. But we can begin to become aware of them. And we can begin to experience purification from idolatry whenever we undergo any kind of significant loss or "stripping." Letting go of anything that we have valued more highly than God leads us in the right direction.

Faithfully,

The Theologian

# Sin

Dear Theologian,

My question is about sin. It is written that Jesus died for our sins, and we are told that our sins are forgiven. But I find that I sin again and again, even after I know that I've been forgiven. What is worse, it is often the same sin that I am committing over and over. I feel that I am "letting the Lord down," after He has forgiven me. How can I go on accepting His forgiveness when I keep repeating my sins?

Burdened by Guilt

Dear Burdened,

You are not the first one to feel this anguish of spirit. The great apostle St. Paul struggled with the same experience of moral inconsistency and failure to live up to his ideals. *"I do not do the good I want, but the evil I do not want is what I do... Wretched man that I am! Who will rescue me from this body of death?"* (Rom 7:19,24)

Repeated sin and renewed forgiveness are found throughout the story of Israel, God's chosen people. Though loved and forgiven again and again, Israel continued to fall away and be unfaithful to the covenant. Some of the prophets compared God to a loving husband whose wife (Israel) was tragically inconsistent in her response to Him. (See, for example, Hosea.)

But in Christ, something utterly new has entered the situation. Immediately after the desperate rhetorical question quoted above, Paul exclaims, *"Thanks be to God through Jesus Christ our Lord!"* (Rom 7:25)

As Paul understands things, God has acted decisively in Christ to reconcile sinful human beings to Himself. (2 Cor 5:19) Christ, though innocent, took upon himself the terrible pain of sin's alienation from God, and laid down his life for the sake of all other human beings. By dying this way, he triumphed over sin and death, and opened up an entirely new way of being human. Paul calls it *"a new creation."* (2 Cor 5:17)

What matters now, is to "be in Christ." This is how Paul regards the condition of those who have been baptized. United with the crucified and risen Christ, they are brought into the closest intimacy with God.

Does this mean that baptized persons no longer commit sins? This is clearly ruled out by experience! Yet we sense correctly that the choice to "be in Christ" is a choice to renounce all evil. This is clearly expressed in the liturgy of Baptism.[34]

In principle, therefore, a newly baptized person should no longer choose evil, should no longer commit sins. But the liturgy of Baptism recognizes that, even though we are engaged in a struggle against evil, we will commit sins. "Will you persevere in resisting evil, and, whenever you fall into sin, repent and return to the Lord? —I will, with God's help." [35]

But aren't we hypocritical in continually seeking forgiveness for the same sins? Shouldn't we show notable improvement, in order to feel "OK" before the loving and forgiving Lord?

We would be insincere in our repentance if we did not truly intend, with all our heart, to do better in the future. Even though past experience may have shown us that we will almost certainly fall into the same sins again, our desire is to "amend our life."

We do, of course, feel the "wretchedness" of failing over and over to live up to our sincere intention of amending our life. Perhaps we begin to realize that we will never be able to present ourselves to God as being fully "satisfactory" or "acceptable" in His sight.

We should sincerely regret our repeated failures, but at the same time acknowledge that we are continually and permanently in need of God's mercy. We have learned from Jesus that God accepts us as we are and loves us as we are. It is not that God approves of our sins. But God approves of us. As we have often heard, God hates sin but loves the sinner.

Perhaps the nearest analogy in our experience is the way a parent may sometimes continue to love and accept a wayward son or daughter. But this comparison falls short, because even a good and loving human parent has only a finite ability to keep on forgiving.

34      Cf. BCP, p. 302
35      BCP, p. 304, emphasis added.

Our difficulty in allowing God to continually forgive our repeated sins may arise from our unconscious projection onto God of our own very limited readiness to forgive. Think of Peter's question to Jesus: *"Lord, if my brother sins against me, how often should I forgive? As many as seven times?"* (Surely you don't expect much more than that, do you?) And recall Jesus' answer: *"Not seven times, but, I tell you, seventy times seven times."* (Mt 18:21-22; see also Lk 17:4)

*"There is therefore now no condemnation for those who are in Christ Jesus."* (Rom 8:1) We do feel sorrow over our repeated sins, but we need not despair over our failures, because God's infinite mercy continues to enfold us. The mercy of God is experienced most fully in our never-ending need for forgiveness.

Faithfully,

The Theologian

# Grace

Dear Theologian,

What is the theological meaning of the word "grace?" I notice that we refer to it often in our prayers and hymns. And when we ask God for "grace," what do we hope to be given?

In Search of Grace

Dear Searcher,

In both the story of Israel and the story of Jesus, the word "grace" conveys a quality of God that has been experienced. It means that God is good, kind and generous to all human beings, blessing them beyond what they could ever "earn" or deserve.

It is not immediately evident to the human mind that "ultimate reality" is gracious. This needs to be discovered through experience. As we human beings live our finite lives in space and time, we reach out in faith to the Infinite. We wonder, sometimes anxiously, about the nature of the ultimate reality on which we depend. Is it to be trusted? Is it to be loved? May we safely abandon ourselves to it? Is God "good"?

The long tradition in which we stand answers these urgent questions with a firm "Yes." We believe that, beginning with the remote figure of Abraham, God has been creating and forming a people to know God's name ("what God is like") and to live in intimate relationship with God. The revelation given to Israel, preserved in the sacred writings of the Hebrew Bible, is summed up in this text from the Book of Exodus:

> "*The LORD said to Moses, '... you have found favor in my sight, and I know you by name.' Moses said, 'Show me your glory, I pray.' And he said, 'I will make all my goodness pass before you.' ... The LORD passed before him, and proclaimed: 'The LORD, the LORD, a God merciful and gracious, slow to anger, and abounding in steadfast love and faithfulness, keeping steadfast love for the thousandth generation.'*" (Ex 33:17-19; 34:6-7)

We Christians believe that the story of Israel culminated in Jesus of Nazareth, in whom we recognize the definitive revelation of "what God is like."

His parables challenged people to believe in a God who is generous and merciful to the undeserving. He acted out the mystery of divine generosity and mercy by accepting and associating with the unacceptable people of his day. He ate and drank with "sinners," and healed the wretched of their physical and emotional disorders. In all this, he was consciously showing the gracious goodness of God, the "in-breaking" of God's blessed "rule" or "kingdom."

But the greatest revelation of God's graciousness came in Jesus' death and resurrection. Only in that final, unexpected "turn" of the story do we receive the ultimate disclosure of what God is truly like, and what we may expect from God.

Out of mankind's tragic rejection of God's love as it was embodied in Jesus, God made a new beginning that went beyond any revelation that had been given before. The No of human beings was overcome by God's decisive Yes.

In the risen Jesus, God was revealed as the One *who gives life to the dead and calls into existence the things that do not exist.* (Rom 4:17) A new possibility for human life was opened to believers, a way of living in trusting intimacy with God, set free from sin and the fear of death.

This is why the New Testament writings are pervaded by a joyous awareness of "grace." St. Paul, in his letters, stresses the gift-quality of the "righteousness" that comes through faith in Christ. No one can earn or deserve God's approval by what they do, but everyone can, by faith, humbly receive the gift of God.

The term "grace" is often used to name the gracious, freely given power of God that enables people to believe, to bear witness, and to serve. This is especially noticeable in the story of the early Church in the Acts of the Apostles.

In a profoundly true sense, "all is gift." To live by this truth is to enter into the peace of God, which passes all understanding. At the same time, we are left free to accept or reject the gift that is constantly being offered. We are not saved without our own responsible involvement in God's purposes.

This is the great paradox that is at the heart of Christian existence. On the one hand, all is grace. On the other hand, we are free and responsible. St. Paul's exhortation to his people at Philippi gives clear expression to both sides of this paradox:

> *"Therefore, my beloved... work out your own salvation with fear and trembling; for it is God who is at work in you, enabling you both to will and to work for his good pleasure."*
> (Phil 2:12-13)

In another place, St. Paul acknowledges the same truth in very personal terms, as he recognizes both his own effort and the surpassing gift of God:

> *"By the grace of God I am what I am, and his grace toward me has not been in vain. On the contrary, I worked harder than any of them—though it was not I, but the grace of God that is with me."* (1 Cor 15:10)

And in our Anglican liturgy we recognize that even our "good works" are enabled by God's grace:

"We humbly beseech thee, O heavenly Father, so to assist us with thy grace, that we may... do all such good works as thou hast prepared for us to walk in."[36]

This brief explanation of the "doctrine" of grace is addressed to the mind. But for all of us there is another, much deeper level of assimilation. We can come to know something "with our heart." This kind of learning comes only through life experience and prayerful reflection. The paradox of grace and freedom, though it can never be resolved by rational thought, can be lived in direct faith-encounter with the living God.

Faithfully,

The Theologian

---

36     Post Communion Prayer, Rite One, BCP p. 339.

# Predestination

Dear Theologian,

It seems to me that the Bible teaches predestination in a number of its books. Of particular importance are the following passages:

> Rom 8:30, *"those whom he predestined he also called; and those whom he called he also justified; and those whom he justified he also glorified."* Eph 1:4, *"he chose us in Christ before the foundation of the world to be holy and blameless before him in love."* Jn 10:28-29, *"I give them eternal life, and they will never perish. No one will snatch them out of my hand. What my Father has given me is greater than all else, and no one can snatch it out of the Father's hand."*

This is to mention only a few of such predestination or election passages. What does this say about our freedom to choose God?

Concerned

Dear Concerned,

"Predestination" is the doctrine that God ordains, from all eternity, who will be saved. Unless one assumes that all will be saved (universal salvation), this doctrine seems to imply that some are predestined to be lost. John Calvin in the sixteenth century made this explicit in his doctrine of "double predestination," according to which, through the sheer will of God, some are eternally ordained to glory, and the rest are ordained to eternal torment.

If the notion of predestination can lead to such an unacceptable view of God's dealing with human beings, why do Christians continue to speak of it at all?

The notion of "predestination" seems to arise from the belief in "divine providence" that is found throughout both the Hebrew Bible and the New Testament. This is the belief that God is sovereign Lord of both nature, human beings, and history. Nothing exists or happens without God's will. God is guiding all things toward the fulfillment of God's purposes.

In the Hebrew Bible, "predestination" as a concept is only hinted at in the image of the "Book of Life" (Ps 69:28, Ex 32:32, Dan 12:1). In the New Testament, however, it is affirmed explicitly in several passages, as your citations show.

In the New Testament, the belief in God's ruling providence over human affairs is taken for granted. It is not surprising, therefore, that some texts speak of God's saving work in Christ in terms of God foreseeing and willing this from all eternity. They affirm "predestination" in the totally positive sense of having been chosen and saved by God from before all time. This does not necessarily mean that others have been predestined to damnation.

But even if one does not draw out the implication that some are predestined to be lost, there remains the problem that you have named. If the just are infallibly predestined to be saved, what room is there for them to choose God?

This points us directly into the central paradox of Christian faith: the paradox of grace and human freedom. The Christian realizes that he or she depends utterly on the grace of God, but also acknowledges personal responsibility for choosing. St. Paul expressed it this way: "...by the grace of God I am what I am, and his grace toward me has not been in vain. On the contrary, I worked harder than any of them —though it was not I, but the grace of God that is with me." (1 Cor 15:10)

Christians affirm both the utter sovereignty of God's grace and the true freedom of human persons to accept or reject God's love. In the words of an Orthodox theologian, such a paradox "testifies to the existence of a mystery beyond which the human reason cannot penetrate. This mystery nevertheless is actualized and lived in religious experience." [37]

The concept of "predestination," therefore, is not to be regarded as a speculative truth that has been somehow discovered and comprehended by human reason. It is a conviction that has grown out of the lived experience of many generations of believers. But it coexists in the Christian mind with the certainty of freedom and moral responsibility, which also arises out of experience.

When we attempt to unify these two convictions in a rational way, we find ourselves at an impasse. We are involved with something too great for our human minds ever to comprehend. We are face-to-face with Mystery. We can and do live in relationship to Mystery, even though we cannot conceptualize it adequately.

37    Sergius Bulgakov, *The Wisdom of God.*

Karl Rahner, the great 20th-century Roman Catholic theologian, maintained that the purpose of good theological thinking is what he called *reductio in mysterium*, that is, to bring a human person again to the awareness of Mystery. At that point, there is no need or room for further thinking or talking, but only for silence and worship.

Faithfully,

The Theologian

# Christmas

Dear Theologian,

I've been getting a lot of greeting cards that say "Happy Holidays" or "Season's Greetings." What happened to "Merry Christmas"? As a matter of fact, why do we still call this holiday season "Christmas"? What does it have to do with Christ?

Old-fashioned Christian

Dear Christian,

The familiar word "Christmas" comes down to us from an earlier age, when people lived by the liturgical calendar and every great feast was observed by attending Mass (the Holy Eucharist). Certain days of the year were designated by "whose" Mass was being celebrated. In such a world of faith, the day of Christ's nativity was naturally called "Christ-Mass" (Old English *Cristes maesse*).

But why do we still use such an explicitly Christian word to designate our secularized winter holiday season? Has the word perhaps lost its original meaning? Does our present-day "Christmas" actually still have anything to do with Christ?

It's a question worth asking, as we experience each year the relentless pressure of Christmas shopping and listen endlessly to Christmas music from Thanksgiving Day until December 25th.

Let's begin with some history. In the earliest period of Christianity there was no firm tradition about the date of Jesus' birth. It was only in the fourth century that the Church began to celebrate the birth of Christ in late December, perhaps in order to counteract the license and debauchery of the pagan festival of Saturnalia, held at the time of the winter solstice (the shortest day of the year). Some have also speculated that the date of December 25 was chosen as a Christian rival to the pagan festival of "the unconquered sun" (*sol invictus*) celebrated on that date.

When missionaries later brought the good news of Christ to the Germanic tribes, they had to adapt the Church's life to a culture very different from the Greco-Roman world in which Christianity had begun.

People in the northern lands traditionally responded to the change of season by celebrating a kind of "winter festival." Evergreens and mistletoe brought life and color into their homes, and a blazing fire (the Yule log) kept away the darkness and bitter cold. It was a time when people gathered to eat and drink, sing and dance, exchange gifts and experience the joy and security of being together. Hence the December celebration of Christ's birth gradually became interwoven with the old Germanic customs, and the folklore of Christmas as we know it began to develop.

Keeping this in mind, we might be able to appreciate better the kind of Christmas celebration that has gradually taken shape here in the United States. In colonial days the observance of Christmas was often raucous and disorderly, marked by carousing and drunkenness. The Puritans wanted to ban it altogether. In the nineteenth century, an effort was made to calm things down by introducing the custom of exchanging cards and gifts and celebrating the warmth and closeness of the family. Charles Dickens' *A Christmas Carol* was influential.

Later in the nineteenth century the myth of Santa Claus and his reindeer became prominent through the influence of a poem, "'T was the Night before Christmas," and a series of vivid illustrations in magazines. Few Americans today are aware of how recently these now omnipresent themes were introduced.

What has resulted is a peculiar mixture of a more or less secular "winter festival" with images of the baby Jesus (with accompanying angels, shepherds, Joseph and Mary, and the wise men from the East). Some of the special music is devoutly Christian, with beloved carols dating from the eighteenth and nineteenth centuries. But much of it simply expresses the various aspects of the winter festival, which now includes the Santa Claus myth.

How is all this to be regarded from the viewpoint of Christian faith? How can some of us still find Christ in the American "Christmas"?

Despite the commercialism and materialism, there are some positive values in our December festival, even when Christian faith is totally absent from it.

People decorate their homes with outdoor lights and set up richly decorated evergreen trees in their living rooms. It's a time to prepare for the gathering of families—by sending greeting cards, buying gifts, laying in a good supply of holiday food and drink, making travel arrangements. "Home for the holidays!" It's a time of special delight for the children in our homes. The tree, the toys, the colored lights, the music, the special food, and the excitement all combine to create a feeling of the magical.

This "winter festival" could be viewed as our human spirit's response to the challenge of cold and darkness. It could be seen as an affirmation of life and warmth and joy, despite the harsh conditions, as people gather out of separate, busy lives in order to be together in a festive spirit, to eat and drink, exchange gifts, and feel the warmth of family.

None of this need be denied or minimized when we add the dimension of Christian faith. For Christ elevates and transforms human nature without destroying it. If we confess Jesus to be the Lord of all things, there is a magnificent depth of meaning to the winter festival, and a reason for joy in the midst of the darkness of human suffering and sin. *"The light shines in the darkness, and the darkness has not overcome it."* (Jn 1:5)

Our human effort to affirm life against the forces of death, to create a warm, cheerful, well-lighted place against the cold and darkness, to celebrate the bonds of family and friendship despite our conflicts and wounds—all this is now undergirded and validated and filled with transcendent power by the everlasting Love which has taken on an earthly, human presence.

In Christ, and because of Him, our celebration of the winter festival can become radiant with the light of God. And our sound human impulses to be of good cheer and to be good to one another are affirmed and empowered by the Grace that has manifested itself in our midst.

Merry Christmas!

The Theologian

# Section 6: Eschatology—the "Last Things"

The "last things" to be treated in this section challenge the rational mind's ability to find firm footing. The topics of Death, Judgment, Heaven and Hell cannot be interpreted in a satisfying way. Yet they are unavoidable.

# Life After Death

Dear Theologian,

What do Christians believe about life after death? What does the Episcopal Church teach about this?

A Troubled Believer

Dear Troubled,

It is impossible to speak or write about death without recognizing that this is an awesome mystery before which the human mind falls silent. None of us know yet what it will be like for us personally to die. As our years increase, we begin at times to think of this, even though we could hardly think seriously of our own death when we were very young. We know what it is like to stand at the graveside of someone else, and as we contemplate the death of others, it looks like a going "into the dark." We believe and hope that it is the entry into everlasting Light, but we cannot know with certainty what is beyond death.

Trying to respond to your question, therefore, is not a matter of providing information about something that is proportioned to our human understanding. We do not have knowledge about "life after death," but we who believe in Christ live with a special kind of hope.

Our hope is expressed this way in the Preface for the Commemoration of the Dead: "To your faithful people, O Lord, life is changed, not ended; and when our mortal body lies in death, there is prepared for us a dwelling place eternal in the heavens." [38]

"Life is changed, not ended." But if it is truly "changed," then we can hardly think merely of some kind of continuation of ordinary life. Whatever we mean by "life after death" must refer to a condition utterly beyond our power to conceive or imagine.

The Church's liturgy for the Burial of the Dead faces honestly the sadness and finality of death, but still sings the song of Easter faith:

38    BCP, p. 380.

"You only are immortal, the creator and maker of mankind; and we are mortal, formed of the earth, and to earth shall we return. For so did you ordain when you created me, saying, 'You are dust, and to dust you shall return.' All of us go down to the dust; yet even at the grave we make our song: Alleluia, alleluia, alleluia." [39]

The Church's paradoxical faith finds powerful expression in the opening anthem of the funeral liturgy—words that have become hallowed in memory through repetition from generation to generation:

"I am the resurrection and the life, saith the Lord;
he that believeth in me, though he were dead,
 yet shall he live;
and whosoever liveth and believeth in me shall never die.
I know that my Redeemer liveth,
and that he shall stand at the latter day upon the earth;
and though this body be destroyed, yet shall I see God;
whom I shall see for myself and mine eyes shall behold,
and not as a stranger." [40]

The paradox involved in Christian hope is here poignantly expressed. "Though he were dead, yet shall he live." "Though this body be destroyed, yet shall I see God." What kind of "life after death" are we to hope for, even though our body is destroyed?

What we hope for is expressed in the creeds by the imagery of "the resurrection of the body and the life everlasting" (Apostles' Creed) or "the resurrection of the dead, and the life of the world to come" (Nicene Creed).

In the Catechism of the Book of Common Prayer an effort is made to explain the meaning of these images:

"Q. What do we mean by the resurrection of the body?

A. We mean that God will raise us from death in the fullness of our being, that we may live with Christ in the communion of the saints.

---

39    BCP, p. 499.
40    BCP, p. 469.

Q. What do we mean by everlasting life?

A. By everlasting life, we mean a new existence, in which we are united with all the people of God, in the joy of fully knowing and loving God and each other." [41]

This form of hope is clearly bound up with the belief that Jesus, who "died our death" is now "risen from the dead." The faith which we profess and celebrate in the face of death is the Easter faith that trusts unconditionally in the God who has raised Jesus from the dead. This faith entrusts the dead to God with grief over their loss but with hope for their eternal joy. In doing this, the mourners also express their own hope for resurrection.

As St. Paul has written,

> "... Christ has been raised from the dead, the first fruits of those who have died. For since death came through a human being, the resurrection of the dead has also come through a human being; for as all die in Adam, so all will be made alive in Christ." (1 Cor 15:20-23)

To believe in God this way enables Christians to regard death with utter realism and at the same time not to despair. In fact, they are even able to rejoice, for they hope to be "with" the risen Lord—whatever that might involve.

Scripture presents this prospect in a simple and deeply moving way. Jesus speaks to his troubled and frightened disciples on the evening before his death:

> "Do not let your hearts be troubled. Believe in God, believe also in me. In my Father's house there are many dwelling places. If it were not so, would I have told you that I go to prepare a place for you? And if I go and prepare a place for you, I will come again and will take you to myself, so that where I am, there you may be also." (Jn 14:1-3)

It is well to keep in mind that—in all this discussion—we are straining human words beyond their ordinary meaning, in order to give voice to the hope which sustains us as believers in Christ. What we say does not provide information, but rather invites to Easter faith.

In Christ,
The Theologian

---

41    BCP, p. 862.

# Praying for the Dead

Dear Theologian:

Why do we pray for the dead? Hasn't their eternal condition been established at the time of their death? If they are in heaven, they don't need our prayers. And if they are in hell, our prayers for them would be futile. What good do we think we can do them by praying for them?

Uncertain

Dear Uncertain,

We need to be humble in our efforts to speak about the dead. Although the Church has developed a doctrine about "the last things" (death, judgment, heaven, and hell), we must recognize the limits of our theological reasoning about such great mysteries.

It is probably best to approach your question from the angle of "Christian hope." (Cf. BCP, pp. 861-862.) Christian faith cannot claim to have any specific knowledge about the state of those who have died. But it does affirm an unshakable trust in the faithfulness of the God who raised Jesus from the dead. Christians live and die, therefore, in the hope of sharing in Christ's resurrection.

In the Church's reflection on this hope, various ideas about the state of the dead have been worked out. The traditional Christian view has been something like the following:

Each person at the time of death enters into "eternity" (a state beyond time) in the relationship to God which has been fashioned through all their choices over a life-time. This relationship can be either "heaven" ("eternal life in our enjoyment of God") or "hell" ("eternal death in our rejection of God"). [42]

"Judgment" is the event by which the person's eternal state is made clear. The Church has developed a distinction between "the particular judgment" of each individual (at death) and "the general judgment" of all human beings at the end of history.

Some Christians imagine that the individual enters immediately into his or her eternal condition at death. Others suppose that the

---

42    BCP, p. 862.

person is "asleep" until the general judgment and the resurrection from the dead. Roman Catholics, moreover, believe in the possibility of an intermediate state of purification after death, for those destined for heaven but not yet ready to enter into the presence of God.

This is the conceptual framework within which your question has a clear logic. Why, indeed, should we pray for the dead if their destiny has already been decided? On the other hand, the Church from the earliest times has always prayed for the dead.

In the Roman Catholic view, of course, it does make sense to pray for the dead because many or even most of them are probably going through the painful purification process that is called "purgatory." As a matter of fact, the theological idea of purgatory is derived partly from the Church's universal practice of praying for the dead.

How do Episcopalians think about the problem? Even though the doctrine of purgatory is formally rejected in the Thirty-Nine Articles,[43] the Catechism of the American Prayer Book seems to envisage some further process of spiritual growth after the point of death: "We pray for [the dead] because we still hold them in our love, and because we trust that in God's presence those who have chosen to serve him will grow in his love, until they see him as he is." [44]

A further element that influences our thinking about this is the doctrine of the Communion of Saints, which affirms that the communion of human persons "in Christ" is not broken even by death. There is a spiritual unity of the living with all those who have gone before them in faith. The great fellowship extends beyond all boundaries of time or place, to include all those who have been or ever will be gathered into Christ.

The Church's firm sense of loving solidarity with those who have gone ahead into the inscrutable mystery of death leads the Church to pray for them just as it prays for the living.

But what does it mean to pray for the living? Are we not entrusting them to the unimaginable greatness and goodness of the One whom Jesus addressed as '"father"? But we cannot do this without at the same time entrusting ourselves totally. Could we not think of praying for the dead along the same lines? Praying for the dead could therefore

---

43    See Article XXII, BCP, p. 872.
44    BCP, p. 862.

be understood as holding them lovingly in our hearts as we make our own radical surrender, in faith, to the incomprehensible mystery of God.

Do we think that our praying for the dead "makes a difference" in the outcome of their earthly pilgrimage? This is beyond our knowing, since it is hidden in the mystery of God's love for the world in Christ. All we are sure of, in faith, is what St. Paul says in Rom 8:31-39.

Picking up on this famous passage, the very last question in the Catechism of the Prayer Book asks, "What, then, is our assurance as Christians?" And the response is: "Our assurance as Christians is that nothing, not even death, shall separate us from the love of God which is in Christ Jesus our Lord. Amen."[45]

Faithfully,

The Theologian

---

45    *Ibid.*

# Heaven, Hell and Eternity

Dear Theologian,

Do we still believe in heaven and hell? I don't hear much preaching about either one, these days, even though both are mentioned in our Prayer Book Catechism. And what about the idea of "eternity"? Are we to imagine anything going on and on, forever?

Somewhat Skeptical

Dear Skeptic,

You're probably right about the scarcity of preaching on heaven and hell (especially the latter). In the past, these words have called up all kinds of vivid imagery which have truly engaged the imagination of the listeners. It has to be said, though, that the images of hell used to make a greater impression on people than the rather tame and bland images of heaven. Hell was certainly to be feared and avoided, if possible, but heaven didn't really seem all that attractive to many people.

Do we still believe in heaven and hell? The Prayer Book Catechism apparently assumes that we do, when it says, as you note: "By heaven, we mean eternal life in our enjoyment of God; by hell, we mean eternal death in our rejection of God."[46] This terse answer introduces also the mysterious concept of eternity which you are asking about. Whatever heaven and hell are, they are to be imagined as "eternal."

It might help to remind ourselves that both "heaven" and "hell" are symbols generated by the human mind to point to something beyond the range of human knowing. They symbolize the ultimate state of human beings beyond death, imagined as the outcome of the way they lived their lives.

What does the symbol "heaven" mean to Christian believers? Certain biblical images come to mind: a beautiful city with streets of gold (the new Jerusalem); thousands and thousands of people worshiping before the throne of God and singing praise; a great dinner

46      BCP, p. 862.

party—a banquet—with all good things to eat and drink, where people are gathered to feast and celebrate forever. The very multiplicity of images reminds us that they are not to be taken literally.

The Catechism says, "Eternal life in our enjoyment of God." But we cannot know what that will be like. It goes beyond our ability to imagine. Scripture says, *"No eye has seen, nor ear heard, nor the human heart conceived, what God has prepared for those who love him."* (1 Cor 2:9)

One way of approaching the great mystery is to begin with our faith in the risen Christ. Although "heaven" is probably to be conceived more as a "state of being" than "location in a particular place," we Christians hope to be "with" the risen Lord—whatever that might involve.

What does the symbol "hell" mean to Christian believers? Putting aside, for a moment, the lurid imagery associated with the word, how can we think about what that symbol points toward?

The Catechism calls it "eternal death in our rejection of God." If "eternal death" were taken to mean simply annihilation, there would be nothing to fear. But if it means, rather, an "eternal" state of utter alienation from all truth, goodness and beauty, it is indeed a fearful prospect.

"Hell," in this conception, would not be thought of as a "place" to which one is sent as a punishment for wrong-doing. Rather, it would be understood as a self-chosen state in which one stubbornly and irrevocably chooses darkness rather than light, nothingness rather than the fullness of being. It would be the constantly chosen absolutizing of self-will, in rejection of God's will.

Is that conceivable? We get a hint of its possibility even now whenever we stubbornly refuse—in either a major or minor way—to be part of God's Kingdom. Some of us know what the alienation from God feels like. One might even say that we get a kind of foretaste of "hell" when we choose to be in that attitude (just as we get a kind of foretaste of "heaven" when we surrender gladly to God's will).

The Church has never taught that any person is actually "in hell." But it has consistently affirmed the possibility of such an outcome of a human life. Some people today are reluctant to consider that possibility, but to rule it out seems to trivialize the seriousness of our human journey with its moral choices.

What is to be said about the notion of "eternity"? Does that mean "going on forever"? Somehow, the prospect of a prolonged existence without any end could be somewhat frightening. We might wonder what it would be like to have even a good thing go on forever and ever.

But is that the right way to think about eternity? Let me suggest another way of thinking about it. "Eternity" does not mean simply time which goes on and on without end. Rather, it means a way of being that does not involve time at all! To be in eternity is just to be "now." No yesterday, no tomorrow. Just "now."

We cannot really imagine that, of course. The closest we can come, perhaps, is to think of a particular "now" in our past life that was full of gladness and love, and imagine that it did not have to slip away into the past. We could "abide" in the fullness of that "now" without any fear of loss. This might give us a hint of what the state called "heaven" might be like.

But how about the state called "hell"? Is it also to be imagined simply as a "now" that does not pass away? Some have preferred to believe in the possibility of someone in that state "changing their mind" and choosing, after all, to be "in heaven" by surrendering to God's will.

The third century Christian theologian Origen thought that God's never-failing love would finally overcome even the most stubbornly resisting heart, so that all would ultimately be reconciled with God. A less optimistic estimate is made by C.S. Lewis in his book *The Great Divorce,* where he imagines that only some would choose to be in heaven rather than stay in hell.

"Believing in" heaven and hell is, finally, not a matter of affirming the existence of some unknowable realities. It is a matter of "believing in God," by entrusting ourselves and all our hopes for ultimate fulfillment to the incomprehensible Mystery that Jesus taught us to call "Abba," while knowing that we are always capable of rejecting that infinite Mercy.

In Christ,
The Theologian

# Rapture

Dear Theologian:

I want to ask about "the rapture." I've been reading a fascinating novel called *Left Behind*, in which millions of people suddenly disappear from the planet. In the story, these are the good Christians who have been snatched up and taken directly to heaven. Those left behind have to cope with the ensuing seven years of "tribulation," during which the Antichrist reigns. What about all this? Is belief in the rapture part of Christian faith? Are we to expect that something like this will actually happen?

Half-Believing

Dear Half-Believing:

A lot of people have read this novel and its series of sequels. For many, it may be just an intriguing fantasy-adventure story, but for others it undoubtedly corresponds to their religious beliefs as evangelical Christians.

What can be said about this, from an Anglican perspective? Do we live in expectation of a literal "rapture," in which certain living persons are taken directly "to heaven" without going through the experience of death?

We need to situate this question in the larger context of Christian hope. From the beginning, Christian faith has been oriented to a future state in which the Kingdom of God would be realized in its fullness. The first generation of believers expected this to happen in the very near future, during their own life-time, at the return of Christ in glory to judge the world. But when the "arrival" (PAROUSÍA) of Christ did not occur as expected, they had to adjust their faith accordingly. In effect, the Church settled down to live in history "for the long haul," but without ever giving up the hope that, in the end, Christ would come again.

Christian faith has never completely lost its "eschatological" character (the orientation to the "end-time" of God's fulfillment), but for many Christians and for long periods of time this expectation has been muted. Strong belief in the imminent end of the world and second coming of Christ tends to revive at times of crisis, widespread suffering, and turmoil in human affairs.

How does "the rapture" of the novels fit in with the hope of Christ's second coming?

There are a couple of texts in the letters of St. Paul which have inspired some to imagine a literal "snatching-up." In 1 Thess 4:13-18 and 1 Cor 15:51-52 Paul is addressing those Christian believers whose hope in the PAROUSÍA had been weakened by seeing fellow-believers die before the Lord had come again. He assures them that the Lord Jesus will return to raise the blessed dead, and that believers who are still alive when Christ comes will then be *"changed"* (1 Cor 15: 51-52) or *"caught up in the clouds together with them to meet the Lord in the air"* and so *"be with the Lord forever."* (1 Thess 4:17)

Christian faith does involve a hope in the ultimate triumph of Christ over all the forces of evil, and his glorious manifestation to all human beings. But no particular interpretation of how or when this might happen is proposed by the Episcopal Church as binding doctrine. Moreover, belief in "the rapture" as imagined in the Left Behind novels has no real basis in Scripture, despite the wide-spread acceptance of this idea.

If we respond in faith to the texts of Scripture cited above (1 Thess 4 and 1 Cor 15), what are we really hoping for? Should we think of some people literally being "snatched up" into an invisible sphere ?

Most basic to this whole discussion is the importance of distinguishing between literal and symbolic language. It is a mistake to take the symbolic texts of Scripture as literal descriptions of this-world events. They hint at what is beyond our human capacity to understand or conceptualize. They point into the inscrutable mystery of God bringing the world to its fullness.

To be "caught up" into God, then, can scarcely be thought of as a spatial movement. Whatever it means, it points to a spiritual event that defies conceptualization. To be a Christian includes hope in the God who comes. But we need not be tied to any particular way of symbolizing or imagining that coming.

Sincerely,

The Theologian

# Section 7:

# Concluding Reflections

As I review the essays in this collection, I recognize that I am always explaining a consistent faith outlook which I consider to be "the faith of the Church" (as I have received and lived it). I am looking at the contours of this ecclesial faith as it guides and patterns the spiritual life of Church members.

What I am doing in this book is a product of my two vocational commitments. It is my identity as priest that finds expression in these essays, as well as my identity as academic theologian. I am drawing upon both my spiritual experience as priest and the expertise in theology I have acquired over many years of advanced studies and teaching.

I wrote all these essays during a period of my life when I was full-time pastor of an Episcopal congregation. In that role I was constantly trying to communicate the faith of the Church to my people in various ways. Weekly preaching was a demanding discipline that required me to ponder deeply the meaning of the doctrines and symbols of that faith, in relation to the concrete life situations of the people I was addressing.

Hence, my interest and motivation in writing the "Dear Theologian" pieces is clearly pastoral. I am addressing Christian believers in order to clarify and enrich their understanding of the faith they profess. The intellectual exposition is directed always toward the living-out of Christian faith in a contemporary mode.

I am aware that my understanding of the faith remains in some ways fundamentally Catholic, because of how deeply and positively I was formed in the Roman communion during the years of renewal following the Second Vatican Council. But it is now in an Anglican context that I attempt to present and explain what I consider to be valid in this heritage.

There is nothing in the least polemical in what I have written here. My purpose has not been to argue about controversial issues which may still mark off various versions of the "one, holy, catholic and apostolic Church." Instead, I have tried to present a consistent, positive interpretation of the Christian faith from my own specific and limited perspective.

This has not taken the form of constructing or defending some grand scheme of systematic theology. Instead, there are many "snapshots" of a coherent theology from the various angles of the questions asked. It's as if the Mystery is far too great and rich to be talked about as a whole, but can only be approached from specific situations of inquiry.

Have I been doing my theologizing in an Anglican manner? Perhaps yes, in the sense of trying always to think and write from what I consider to be the Catholic faith of the ages. This kind of writing is pastoral and even devotional at times, precisely by being a serious effort to clarify the meaning and implications of Catholic beliefs and doctrines.

It includes careful intellectual exposition not for its own sake, but for the sake of living the Christian faith in all its richness. The impulse to explain and understand better arises out of a lived ecclesial faith, and in that sense is, indeed, "faith seeking (and offering) understanding." A more adequate and authentic understanding can, in turn, enrich and deepen the lived faith.

I have attempted in the Introduction to let the reader know, in a general way, "where I am coming from" ecclesiastically and theologically. Here, at the conclusion of the book, I just want to touch briefly on some themes that are quite prominent in the collection.

In all these essays I am drawn continually to the central reality of the Church's faith: Jesus the Crucified and Risen One. In the words of the Eucharistic liturgy, it is "through him and with him and in him" that we relate to the Father and, indeed, are drawn into the life of the Holy Trinity.

My treatment of what theologians call Christology is very limited in scope, but I am affirming what the Church has come to define and proclaim about Jesus the Christ. Therefore, in the essays of Section

147

Two ("The Mystery of Christ") I try to show the importance for Christian faith life of the doctrines of the Incarnation and the Paschal Mystery, as well as the significance of praying "through Christ." I have also found it necessary to ponder deeply the significance of Christ's resurrection for the Christian's conception of God and for the ongoing life of faith in a world where everyone eventually dies.

Faith in the Holy Spirit is basic to the consideration of all the topics in this collection. In particular, the essay on "Believing in the Holy Spirit" is foundational for whatever is to be said about the Church.

At the center of the Church's communal life is the mystery of Jesus the Christ, crucified and risen and forever present to the world in the power of the Holy Spirit. Each individual member of the fellowship [KOINONÍA] of Jesus Christ has his or her own unique involvement with him, but always as a member of the corporate mystery that is his Body in this world.

Hence, initiation into the Church is of crucial importance for coming to live "in Christ." And growth in the Christ life involves ongoing participation in the Church's liturgical and sacramental life. The Holy Eucharist has a prominent place in my theological understanding, as shown in the several essays about different aspects of this central symbolic ritual of Christian faith. In fact, much of what I would want to affirm about living the Christian faith could be articulated by making explicit the manifold meanings of the Eucharistic celebration.

In my understanding, the Church is always visible in history (not merely an invisible spiritual fellowship), but I recognize the inescapable diversity of faith expression in its different cultural "incarnations." I do not regard any one of the present versions of Church as the sole valid embodiment of this mystery. But I do affirm the urgent need to seek "communion" among its various manifestations.

I regard Church history as the persistence of a "living tradition" across many generations, despite distortions and errors. This tradition had its beginnings in the spiritual experience of Jesus' disciples after his death and their conviction that, though crucified and dead, he was "risen" and present in their lives and in the affairs of this world.

I consider the Scriptures of the New Testament to be the normative written expression of the living tradition, near the time of its beginning. And I view the history of doctrine as the unfolding and re-understanding—again and again—of the mystery that is witnessed to in the Scriptures.

I regard change and development as normal and necessary for the continuation of the living tradition into ever-different cultural environments over the course of history. It was the renewal of the Roman Catholic Church at the time of the Second Vatican Council that enabled me to take such a view of continuity though change. What seemed then to be happening was a fresh conceptualization of the abiding truths of Roman Catholicism, accompanied by new and more appropriate forms for expressing the ancient faith. For those of us who lived through those years, it was an experience of new life that was faithful to the inherited legacy of the Church.

The work of theologians was instrumental in bringing about the renewed forms of Church life that were created by the Council. Insofar as I was aware of their contribution I felt confirmed in my desire to serve the Church as a theologian.

* * *

The enterprise of Christian theology is an ongoing dialogue, with no final account that could ever be considered fully adequate. What I have written here is only a limited but honest account by one theologian. If it helps any fellow believers in their lives of faith, it will have served its purpose.

# Appendix: Some Anglican Questions

These two questions are of interest primarily to Anglican Christians. They may, however, help any reader to assess better the point of view from which the questions in this book are treated.

# What Is Anglicanism?

Dear Theologian,

I'm confused by the present situation among the Churches that call themselves Anglican. Different groups seem to understand this label in different ways, and some of them want to exclude some other Anglican Churches from full communion. Can you answer a simple question? What is "Anglicanism?" Can it be defined? How can it be recognized?

An Anglican (I think!)

Dear Anglican,

Your question is very relevant to our present tensions and disagreements, but it is far from easy to answer satisfactorily.

One approach would be simply historical and descriptive. "Anglicanism" could then be defined as the faith, practice and spirit of the Churches of the Anglican Communion. And these Churches, as we know, are all descended from the Church of England as it emerged from the turbulent years of the Reformation.

This kind of identification of Anglicanism lacks, however, any depth of theological understanding. As Paul Avis asks,

> "Is the faith, practice and spirit of the Churches of the Anglican Communion merely a product of the accidents of history, a legitimization, for reasons of expediency, of the way things have happened to turn out?... Or is Anglicanism possibly the embodiment of some genuine ecclesiological truth or principle with some degree of abiding relevance and with something of value to offer to the whole Church?" [47]

I offer you here my own understanding of what is distinctive (and valuable) in the typically Anglican way of thinking about the mystery revealed in Christ and his Church.

[47] Paul Avis, "What is Anglicanism," in *The Study of Anglicanism*, revised ed., edited by Stephen Sykes, John Booty, & Jonathan Knight (Minneapolis: Fortress Press, 1998), p. 459.

A good starting-point is the thought of Richard Hooker (1554-1600), who is generally recognized as the seminal thinker of the Anglican tradition. What we can learn from Hooker is a thoughtful, balanced way of "doing theology" in the Anglican style, holding in creative interplay Scripture, reason, and the living tradition of the Church.

It is helpful to consider first Hooker's fundamental spiritual and theological vision. A reliable guide to this is John Booty, who spent many years immersed in the study of Hooker's writings:

> "In any definition of Anglicanism based on Hooker's theology, we begin not with the three- or four-legged stool, not with the Quadrilateral, not with The Book of Common Prayer, not with tea at four and sherry before dinner, and not with comprehensiveness and fundamentals, but with wholeness (interdependence, mutual participation, union, and communion). That is to say, we begin with God, of whom all comes, toward whom all tends, by whom all is sustained—God who is revealed in nature and in history, through Israel and preeminently through the Jew chosen of God out of whom the Church was born." [48]

In such contemplative openness to the Mystery, Hooker recognizes the many and various ways that God's self-revelation is mediated to us. In contrast to the narrow biblicism of the Puritans against whom he is arguing, he has a broad, open, and generous way of attending to "the Wisdom of God."

> "His insistence upon wisdom, communicating in innumerable ways, indicates the necessity of openness to wisdom as she teaches us through nature as well as Scripture, through the wisdom of the ancients both religious and pagan, through philosophers as well as rabbis, through science and art, not without questioning and not without expectation. Indeed, 'to detract from the dignitie'

---

48     John E. Booty, *Reflections on the Theology of Richard Hooker* (Sewanee, Tenn.: University of the South Press, 1998), p. 187.

of wisdom, come whence it may, 'were to injurie even God himselfe, who being that light which none can approach unto, hath sent out' a dazzling host of 'lights whereof we are capable, even as so many sparkls resembling the bright fountain from which they rise.'" [49]

Here, at the very beginning of the distinctively Anglican tradition, is an expression of that openness to truth from all sources which is a hallmark of Anglicanism. Moreover, Hooker is explicit in affirming the role of reason in appropriating and understanding God's self-revelation. As one scholar puts it,

"[In Hooker's thought] ... reason is defended as not only presupposed for an accurate understanding of Scripture but as competent to determine a broad range of issues not explicitly covered in Scripture. Hooker's unwillingness to have the Bible used as a source of ahistorical, unambiguous proof texts for dogmatic solutions to all problems is typical of later Anglican thought." [50]

Different parties within Anglicanism have tended to emphasize one particular source of authority, sometimes to the neglect of others. In somewhat oversimplified fashion, we usually say that the Catholic strand of Anglicanism stresses tradition, the Protestant strand stresses Scripture, and the Liberal stresses reason and experience.

The ideal of Anglican theological method would be to hold all three (or four) of these in dialectical and creative tension. This, of course, is more easily said than done, as we know from our present conflicts.

"What is required is not an exhausted and hostile state of noncommunication, but the enduring of the tension in the confidence that truth will emerge from the dialogue... What is required by the very nature of the dialogue is not compromise for the sake of peace, but comprehension for the sake of truth." [51]

---

49    *Ibid.*, p. 189.
50    A.S. McGrade, "Reason," in *The Study of Anglicanism*, revised ed., edited by Stephen Sykes, John Booty, & Jonathan Knight (Minneapolis: Fortress Press, 1998), p. 115.
51    William J. Wolf, "Anglicanism and its Spirit" in *The Spirit of Anglicanism* edited by William J. Wolf, John E. Booty and Owen C. Thomas. (Morehouse-Barlow, 1979), pp. 153-154.

This last quote refers to another key concept in discussions of Anglicanism—"comprehensiveness." This, of course, can be misunderstood to mean "anything goes." But here is a clarifying statement from the Lambeth Conference of 1968:

> "Comprehensiveness demands agreement on fundamentals, while tolerating disagreement on matters in which Christians may differ without feeling the necessity of breaking communion. In the mind of an Anglican, comprehensiveness is not compromise. Nor is it to bargain one truth for another. It is not a sophisticated word for syncretism. Rather it implies that the apprehension of truth is a growing thing: we only gradually succeed in 'knowing the truth.'... Comprehensiveness implies a willingness to allow liberty of interpretation, with a certain slowness in arresting or restraining exploratory thinking.... For we believe that in leading us into the truth the Holy Spirit may have some surprises in store for us in the future as he has had in the past." [52]

Much more would need to be said about the topic you have raised. But perhaps this much will be of some help in trying to assess just how "Anglican" are the various voices in our Church today.

Faithfully,

The Theologian

---

[52]     *The Lambeth Conference* 1968 , pp. 140-41.

# What Do Episcopalians Believe?

Dear Theologian,

When people ask me what the Episcopal Church expects its members to believe, I'm not sure how to answer them. And when people accuse our Church of being vague and uncertain about its beliefs, I don't know how to refute this. Where do I look? Who decides, in our Church, what we are to believe? Are there any "norms" for believing?

Perplexed Episcopalian

Dear Perplexed,

It is true that in our Church there is no "highest court of appeal" for what is to count as orthodox Christian faith, nor is there any single comprehensive and authoritative statement of what is to be believed. In these respects, our form of Church life is in sharp contrast to the Roman Catholic Church. But this is not to say that we have no idea of how and what we believe.

When we Episcopalians are asked to give an account of our beliefs, we have a "stock answer" that is often given. We quote the Latin tag, *"lex orandi, lex credendi"* ("the law of praying is the law of belief"). And we go on to say that our way of believing is to be discovered by considering the ways in which we pray. Our beliefs, we maintain, are implicit in the liturgical forms of worship that we follow, as set down in the Book of Common Prayer.

Seeking to understand this principle leads into a reflection on the relationship of liturgical worship and theological formulations (doctrines).

The liturgical worship of the Church, on the deepest level, is the Spirit-created, Spirit-guided expression of the living faith of its members. This is experienced in common when the baptized gather for liturgical prayer and worship, in humble openness to the Spirit-inspired symbols and metaphors of Sacred Scripture.

The liturgical worship of the Church has grown and developed over the centuries, and has found expression in various ways. These traditions must be both treasured faithfully and continually renewed in relation to the culture of every time and place in which the Church lives.

When Thomas Cranmer created the first Book of Common Prayer, he drew upon various liturgical traditions available to him at the time (Latin, Greek Orthodox, Lutheran and others). He adapted this traditional material to his time and place, to provide for the Church of England a faithful contemporary set of liturgical forms.

The regular use of the 1549 Prayer Book and its later revisions has formed generations of English-speaking worshipers in their spirituality and piety. As one scholar comments, "The texts which are heard and prayed, according to the Book of Common Prayer, inform profoundly the Christian self-understanding and systematic theological reflection of Anglicans." [53]

In a sense, liturgical prayer and worship may be regarded as the "primary theology" of the Church. It is lived without necessarily being examined intellectually or reflected upon.

The task of "secondary theology" is to think about this "lived theology" in a rational, critical way. It attempts to correlate the faith-understanding embodied in the liturgical texts with the culture of a particular time and place. In doing so, it can—when successful—articulate the inherited faith of the Church in ways that connect meaningfully with the life experience of believers.

Moreover, this kind of critical and creative intellectual work—informed by knowledge of and close attention to both Scripture and Church tradition(s)—can and must at times lead to a re-working of the forms of worship themselves, in order to express a new and more "appropriate" understanding of the mysteries of Christian faith.

A case in point is the 1979 American Book of Common Prayer. Some critics of this revision have objected to its "new theology." Louis Weil concedes the point that the 1979 Prayer Book does embody a theology different in certain ways from that implicit in the 1928 Prayer Book. But he justifies this as legitimate and appropriate.

> "The new rites reflected significant theological changes, virtually all of them related to a recovery of a more biblical understanding of the nature of the Church

---

53    W. Taylor Stevenson, "Lex Orandi—Lex Credendi" in *The Study of Anglicanism*, revised ed., edited by Stephen Sykes, John Booty, & Jonathan Knight (Minneapolis: Fortress Press, 1998), p. 189.

as this touched such basic issues as Christian initiation, the Eucharist, and the role of the ordained ministry in relation to other ministries. In other words, the sacramental and liturgical study of the past several decades had gradually shaped a new mentality, and the eventual effect was to create pressure within the Church that its liturgical rites be more honestly expressive of the faith to which they witness." [54]

This seems to be a kind of reversal of the *"lex orandi, lex credendi"* principle. In this case a new way of believing (that is, a new theological mentality) appears to have led to changes in the community's way of praying (its liturgical forms).

Perhaps, therefore, we need to recognize that there is a kind of reciprocal relationship between liturgical worship and theological understanding. They influence one another at different times. Moreover, we have to acknowledge that there is growth, change and development in both theological understanding and liturgical worship.

To return now to your original question, how can we know what the Episcopal Church believes? If one accepts the principle of *"lex orandi, lex credendi"* as valid, then it seems that the question must be answered through careful theological study of the texts of the Book of Common Prayer, in order to make explicit and reflective the faith-understanding contained implicitly in the prayers and liturgical forms.

In principle, of course, it is the regular liturgical worship itself that should form the faith of the participants. But the liturgy, if not properly understood or deeply appreciated, has little effect on people's spirituality. In fact, there is also a need for explicit theological instruction, especially in order to bring out the full meaning and implications of the liturgical prayers and actions.

One might, then, expect that theological study and teaching would play an important part in the Christian formation of Episcopalians. But is this the case? Those who are troubled by the apparent vagueness and superficiality sometimes noticed in our Church are perhaps feeling the lack of solid theological teaching.

What are we to do when theologians differ in their interpretations of Prayer Book faith? On the one hand, as we know, there is no highest instance of authority in the Episcopal Church or the Anglican

---

54    Louis Weil, "The Gospel in Anglicanism," in *The Study of Anglicanism*, revised ed., edited by Stephen Sykes, John Booty, & Jonathan Knight (Minneapolis: Fortress Press, 1998), p. 61.

Communion that could articulate a single, binding interpretation of the faith. On the other hand, the "unformulated" quality of Anglican faith-life allows for a rich plurality of understandings and spiritualities to co-exist in the same communion. It does not absolutize particular formulations in a way that shuts off further growth in understanding.

Is this a happy state of affairs? For very many people, definitely not, since they have a strong need for unambiguous, authoritative teaching on every aspect of Christian faith. For some others, however, the Anglican ethos allows for a welcome freedom in seeking to understand the faith that is being celebrated liturgically according to the established norms of the Book of Common Prayer.

Faithfully,

The Theologian